Michael's

THE NEW GUIDE

CYPRUS

GW00507702

THE NEW GUIDE

Michael's

CYPRUS

Managing Editor
Michael Shichor

Series Editor
Amir Shichor

INBAL TRAVEL INFORMATION LTD.

Inbal Travel Information Ltd.
P.O.Box 1870 Ramat Gan 52117
Israel

©1995-6 edition
All rights reserved

The publishers have done their best to ensure the accuracy and currency of all information contained in this guide; however, they can accept no responsibility for any errors and/or inaccuracies found.

Intl. ISBN 965-288-120-1

Text: Yoram Ya'acovi
Graphic design: Michel Opatowski
Cover design: Bill Stone
Photography: Anat Ofri
Photo editor: Shmulik Weiss
Editorial: Sharona Johan, Or Rinat
D.T.P.: Irit Bahalul, Michael Michelson
Maps: Rina Waserman, Roni Kinderman
Printed by Havatzelet Press Ltd.

Sales in the UK and Europe:
Kuperard (London) Ltd.
9 Hampstead West
224 Iverson Road
London NW6 2HL

Distribution in the UK and Europe:
Bailey Distribution Ltd.
Learoyd Road
New Romney
Kent TN28 8X

U.K. ISBN 1-85733-122-2

CONTENTS

INTRODUCTION

CYPRUS

TABLE OF MAPS

Preface

Cyprus, the majestic island in the eastern Mediterranean, acts as a mirror reflecting the historical vagaries of this part of the world – from the Egyptians to the Persians, and from the Romans to the Byzantine Empire. Its diversed and complicated history is reflected in the unsolved conflict between the Greek and Turkish populations living on the island – each contributing to its character and beauty.

Many Europeans find Cyprus an ideal holiday destination. It is blessed with beautiful beaches and moderate temperament, typical of its weather and people, as is appropriate to a Mediterranean island. What's more, the fast development of its infrastructure promises visitors a pleasant and convenient holiday.

We have devoted the major part of this guide to Greek Cyprus. Since the partition of the Island in 1974, the Greek part, which accounts for two thirds of the entire island, has enjoyed accelerated economic and tourist development, and most tourists visiting Cyprus visit this part. The Turkish side, on the other hand, has a poor infrastructure and can cater primarily to day-trippers residing on the Greek side of the island. At the end of the guide you'll find a special chapter devoted to the Turkish side.

We trust that with our guide's help you'll discover a Cyprus beyond beaches and hotels, a Cyprus rich in history, a Cyprus of mountains dotted with monasteries and forests, villages and hamlets. We hope that you will experience Cyprus as a peaceful island in a sea of modern pulsating life.

Michael Shichor

Using this Guide

In order to reap maximum benefit from the information in this guide, we advise the traveller to carefully read the following passage. The facts contained in this guide were compiled to help the tourist find his or her way around and to ensure that he enjoys his stay to the upmost.

The Introduction provides details which will help you make the early decisions and arrangements for your trip. We suggest that you carefully review the material, so that you will be more organized and set for your visit. Upon arrival in Cyprus, you will feel more familiar and comfortable with the country.

The suggested routes are arranged according to geographical areas, a system that allows for an efficient division of time and ensures a thorough knowledge of each region. More so, this guide will direct you to unexpected places that you may not have heard of and did not plan to visit.

The chapters on main cities include maps and indexes of sites that will help you find your way. On reaching the cities, the guide will direct you to recommended accommodation, restaurants and entertainment places.

The rich collection of maps covers the tour routes in great detail. Especially prepared for this book, they will certainly add to the efficiency and pleasure of your exploration of Cyprus.

To further facilitate the use of this guide, we have included a detailed index. It includes all the major sites that are mentioned throughout the book. Consult the index to find something by name and it will refer you to the place where it is mentioned in greatest detail.

During your visit you will see and experience many things – we have therefore left several blank pages at the back of the guide. These are for you, to jot down those special experiences from people and places, feelings and significant happenings along the way.

Because times and cities are dynamic, an important rule of thumb when travelling should be to consult local sources of information. Tourists are liable to encounter certain inaccuracies in this guide, and for this we apologize.

In this guide we have tried to present updated information in a way which allows for an easy, safe and economical visit. For this purpose, we have included a short questionnaire and will be most grateful for those who will take the time to complete it and send it to us.

Have a pleasant and exciting trip – Bon Voyage!

Upon sending this guide to print, we've learnt that the Cypriot authorities decided on a new policy aimed at unifying the different pronunciations of place names in keeping with the original Greek. Thus Nicosia, the capital, has become Lefkosia, etc. The visitor may see signs bearing both names – the Greek (new), and the former, better known name, in brackets.

Cyprus – the birthplace of Venus; the first stopover of many an ancient wanderer, from Greece or Turkey, from Egypt or Syria; the battle ground of gods – Assyrian and Egyptian, Persian and Roman, Christian and Moslem – for more than forty centuries. Visitors, conquerors and looters of past centuries have left the imprint of their loves and hates, their dreams and fears, their happiness and tears on this little island.

You will not witness the rebirth of Venus. You will not hear the Crusader trumpets embarking toward the Holy Land. And you will not see the blood and tears of Othello and Desdemona. Yet, there is much to enjoy: a splendid array of beaches; modern and inexpensive hotels, against a backdrop of medieval hamlets; some of the most famous wines in history; pine forests and olive groves and lots of ancient vineyards; ruins of forts and temples, monasteries and churches, baths and theatres...

You will enjoy a unique atmosphere of east mixed with west, of mingled pride and patience, of legendary history and of historic legends.

PART ONE –
GETTING TO KNOW CYPRUS

A Long History in Brief

The history of Cyprus begins almost eight thousands years ago. All the early seafaring peoples of the eastern Mediterranean have left their mark on the island: ancient Egypt and Greece, Alexander the Great, the Phoenicians, the Assyrians, Persia, Rome, the Byzantine Empire, the Crusaders, Venice, the Ottomans, the British – all these and more conquered and ruled the island and its people over the centuries. After winning its independence in 1974, Cyprus found itself divided in two, after a brief but cruel civil war, with the northern region affiliated with Turkey and the southern region with Greece.

The amphitheatre at Curium, dating back to the 2nd century BC

ANCIENT TIMES
The earliest signs of human settlement date from the **Neolithic Period**, in the sixth millennium BC, of which remains have been found in several hamlets; the most ancient finds are Choirokoitia, halfway between Nicosia and Limassol. Findings of imported stoneware objects clearly point to trade contacts with the Anatolian population. The earthenware and copper objects discovered in Erimi (near Limassol) and in Souskiou (near Pafos) date from the **Chalcolithic Period** (3rd millennium BC).

During the **Bronze Age** (2300-1800 BC), the Cypriots farmed the land, worshiped a bull-shaped fertility god and a death god symbolized by a snake, practices picked up from their ties with overseas neighbours in Egypt and in Asia Minor.

The **Middle Bronze Age** (1800-1600 BC) is best represented in Eastern Cyprus (in Kalopsida), during which Cyprus came into close contact with the Greek Islands.

During the **Late Bronze Age** (1600-1050 BC) the Mycaeneans swept across the Aegean Sea, conquered Cyprus and settled along its eastern and southern shores, building several new towns and harbours. The discovery of rich copper mines provided Cyprus with new wealth with which it bought peace from its more powerful neighbours and paid tribute to the Egyptian Kings.

Toward the end of the 13th century BC many hamlets began to grow into small towns, complete with walls; temples and public buildings were constructed; Greek customs and culture were slowly adopted throughout the island.

At the beginning of the 1st millennium BC a terrible earthquake shook the island and razed all its cities. Centuries later the ancient centres were slowly rebuilt, often with new names. During this period (the **Iron Age**) the Phoenicians settled along the southern plain; their presence is documented by the ruins of a great temple to their goddess Astarte.

THE ASSYRIAN, EGYPTIAN AND ROMAN RULE

The Assyrians conquered Cyprus in 709 BC and held it until 560 BC, when they were ousted by the Egyptians. The new conquerors left the local Cypriot kings in power, demanding an annual tribute in gold and copper. When Cyprus fell to the Persian Empire (525 BC), the local kings were allowed to remain in power, so long as taxes and tributes continued to flow. The fiscal yoke was so heavy that the Cypriots staged several rebellions, repeatedly repressed with

A mosaic floor, decorating the archaeological site of Curium

cruelty. However, Cyprus' independent spirit survived, and its folk zealously maintained their Greek cultural orientation.

In 333 BC the island was conquered by Alexander the Great, but in 294 BC, after struggles among the king's successors, Cyprus was annexed to Egypt by Ptolomeus I, who ruled Cyprus through an appointed Governor. Cyprus became independent in 109 BC, when Ptolomeus IX, threatened by his mother Cleopatra, was forced to flee Egypt. He took refuge in Cyprus and appointed himself the King of Cyprus. Rome put an end to the Ptolomaean rule in 58 BC, and under the legendary "Pax

Ruins of the ancient Micenean settlement that was founded three thousand years ago

Romana" Cyprus enjoyed a new period of peace and prosperity, as witnessed by the ruins of several highways, aqueducts and theatres.

St. Paul brought the message of Christianity to Cyprus; the Roman Governor Sergius had him lashed and flagellated, but ended up embracing the new faith himself. Paul set up ten bishoprics in the main towns. The local church was headed by the Archbishop of Salamis.

At Curium

In 331 Cyprus became a province of the Byzantine Empire within the Antiochian administration. The local Church, however, maintained its autonomy.

In the 6th Century Cyprus became dependent upon Constantinople; under Justinianus' rule Cyprus enjoyed a new wave of prosperity, witnessed by the many beautiful mosaics, the remains of which can still be admired today.

THE ISLAMIC-BYZANTINE CONFLICT

When Islam began to spread throughout the southern shores of the Mediterranean, Byzantine Cyprus was doomed. In 647 the Caliph of Baghdad imposed new taxes and tributes, and a few years later an Arab Praesidium was set up on the island. The conflict continued for about three centuries, with several invasions from north and south.

In 965 the Byzantine Emperor, Nicaphoros II conquered the island, establishing it as his front against Islam. The Crusaders landed in Cyprus to prepare themselves for the last leg of their journey. Christianity launched its campaigns against Antioch and Tripoli (Syria) from Cyprus. Time after time the Syrians retaliated, destroying the land and slaughtering its people. In 1191 Richard the Lionheart, at the head of a third crusade, conquered Cyprus almost overnight. Today's major centres, Nicosia, Limassol and Famagusta, date from his time.

THE LUSIGNAN DYNASTY

Richard gave Cyprus to Guy de Lusignan, a French nobleman who aspired to the crown of Jerusalem. Three years later, in 1194, Guy died and his brother Aimery took over the newly founded feudal Kingdom of Cyprus, swearing allegiance to the Holy Roman Empire. All lands and properties of the Greek Orthodox Church were confiscated in favour of the Catholic Church.

The Greek peasants of Cyprus lived in great poverty, deprived of freedom. During the next century Cyprus remained a faithful ally of the Kingdom of Jerusalem, and served as the main strategic base for the crusades.

After a period of strife and rebellion, Cyprus once again made a quick recovery, becoming one of the most prosperous trade centres of the Eastern Mediterranean, exporting silk, sugar and spices to Europe. Imposing Gothic Cathedrals were built in Famagusta, Nicosia and elsewhere.

The Lusignan Dynasty ended in 1369, with the murder of King Pierre at the hands of his barons, and for the next century Cyprus passed from one conqueror to the next. Genoa conquered it, Egypt sacked it. Thanks to an alliance between James II and the

A Byzantine jug

Venetian Doges, the island became a Venetian fief, for close to a century. Venetian palaces lined the main streets of Famagusta and St. Mark's Lion stood at the entrance of all Cyprus' main seaports.

After a long struggle between Venice and the Ottoman Empire over trade routes with

the East, Venice was finally defeated and Cyprus fell into Ottoman hands in 1575.

THE OTTOMAN RULE

The new rulers brought the Greek Orthodox Church back to Cyprus; the Orthodox Archbishop was also appointed Head of State. Feudal servitude was abolished, but the heavy taxes imposed on farmers and peasants did little to improve their former condition.

The next two centuries were an epoch of great poverty, drought and pestilence. Frequent rebellions were quelled by the Ottoman rulers, who did not hesitate to execute even the Archbishop himself. Turkish soldiers were granted lands confiscated from the rebels (sowing the seeds of the local Greek-Turkish conflict, which

The statue of the Archbishop Makarios affront the Archbishopric Palace in Nicosia

in the 1970s' culminated in civil war – and the subsequent partitioning of Cyprus).

In 1878 Turkey signed an agreement, granting Cyprus to Great Britain, in return for British support against Russia.

BRITISH RULE

In 1914 Cyprus was officially granted the status of a Crown Colony, and as such became involved in the First World War, on the side of Great Britain, France, Italy and later the United States. In 1915 Great Britain offered Cyprus to Greece, on condition that Greece join the Allies. But Greece joined the fighting only in 1917, and after the war the Allies found reason not to honour their pledge.

For the Cypriots, however, annexation to Greece had become the dream of "Enosis", and the British were repeatedly forced to use arms to repress the frequent rebellions.

During the Second World War, several thousand Cypriots served in the British Army; others found themselves fighting the Nazi invaders from the peaks of Cyprus' mountains. In 1950, after a new wave of strife over "Enosis", annexation to Greece was finally sanctioned by plebiscite. Greece attempted to force implementation of the vote at the United Nations, but Great Britain and Turkey stalled the issue.

At a church in Lefkara

In 1955 Colonel Grivas, a Cypriot born colonel in the Greek Army, founded the EOKA, a sort of "People's Army for Enosis", and Archbishop Makarios gave Enosis his full support. The London Conference, held some weeks later, in which London, Athens and Ankara sought a mutually acceptable solution , ended in failure. Relations between Greece and Turkey became extremely strained. In 1956 the Suez crisis provided Britain with justification to strengthen its local garrison.

Martial law was declared; Makarios and his deputy were deported to the Seychelles Islands. In 1957 they were pardoned, in exchange for an EOKA declaration of ceasefire. EOKA, however, resumed the fight barely one year later.

On 11 February 1959, when it became apparent that Enosis could not be eradicated, Great Britain, Turkey and Greece joined in conference at Zürich and finally granted Cyprus its independence.

INDEPENDENCE
On 16 August 1960, Cyprus officially declared its independence within the British Commonwealth. The Turkish minority (about 18% of the population) was granted 30% representation in Parliament and in the Administration, as well as 40% of the Armed Forces and the office of Deputy President, with veto rights. Great Britain was allowed to maintain its naval bases, in return for its pledge to guarantee Cyprus' independence.

The honeymoon only lasted for a few years. The structure of an administration with dual foundations caused renewed strife. In 1963 the parties came to blows, which grew into a full scale civil war, ending only with the intervention of a United Nations peace force. The peacemakers set up a dividing line between Greeks and Turks, cutting the capital Nicosia in two. This line became the border of two separate political entities: Greek Cyprus and Turkish Cyprus.

The two parent States repeatedly found themselves on the brink of war. The central administration lost its power. The Turkish representatives abandoned their Parliamentary seats and the Deputy President resigned.

When a military junta overthrew the democratic government of Greece, a rift also appeared among Cypriot Greeks. Archbishop Makarios supported democracy; Grivas favoured the junta. The Archbishop's followers took up arms against Grivas' troops.

WAR AND PARTITION
In 1974 a coup brought the extreme right to power, supported by units of the Greek Army. Makarios was ousted; the new president, Nikos

Sampson, lasted less than a week. His successor, Glafkos Clerides, was not recognized by the Turks, whose army invaded the island from the north, conquering one third of its territory, to the Morphou-Nicosia-Famagusta line (the so-called Attila Line). A ceasefire was declared; 200,000 Greeks, residents of the Turkish zone, crossed the line toward the west, and the Turks living in the Greek zone crossed in the opposite direction. The Turkish zone unilaterally declared its own independence.

The situation today is practically the same as it was in 1975. The Western Zone calls itself (in Greek) Kipriaki Democratia; the Eastern Zone calls itself the Turkish Republic of Northern Cyprus (in Turkish Kuzey Kibris Türk Cumhuriyeti). Each side has its own President, Parliament and Cabinet. There are no ties whatsoever between the two.

In official maps published by the two sides, the same localities have different names: Greek Famagusta appears, in Turkish maps, as Gazi Maguza; Nicosia appears as Lefkosa – and so on.

Geography

Cyprus is an island in the Eastern Mediterranean, 40 miles south of Turkey and 60

Vineyards cover the southern slopes of the Troodos Mountains

miles west of Syria. It is the third largest island in the Mediterranean, after Sicily and Sardinia. It covers an area of 3,572 square miles; its maximum east-west spread is 128 miles; north-south 75 miles. Its shores run along about 450 miles.

The island is of Myocenic tectonic origin, separated from the mainland in the epoch of Asia Minor and the Peloponesian islands.

Its origins are reflected in its three main regions: the Troodos Mountains in the West, the Central Mesaoria Plain and the Northern Chain of the Kyrenia Mountains. The Kyrenia Plain in the North, and the hills of the Coastal Plain in the South, complete the geographic structure of the island.

The **Troodos Mountains** cover the south-western quadrant of the island, and are volcanic in character. Its highest peak, Mt. Olympos, soars to a height of 6,403 feet. The chain covers an area of close to 1000 square miles.

Its northern, granitic ridge is steep and barren; its southern hills are calcareous in nature, and crisscrossed by a net of seasonal water beds. The main divide runs from east to west.

Northern Troodos farming is limited to small lots and parcels. Extensive vineyards and orchards are only found on the slopes of the southern hills. The main industrial branch is tourism; the summer climate is pleasantly cool, and in winter the slopes offer some adequate ski runs.

The **Mesaoria Plain** is the heart of Cyprus. Wide, fertile farmland covers the Troodos foothills in the south and the Kyrenia range in the north, and down to the eastern and

The fishermen's harbour at Polis

western Mediterranean beaches. The main river of Cyprus, the Pedieos, crosses the plain from south-west to north-east, providing farmers with ample irrigation water. The main agricultural produce is grain and citrus.

Four of the six major urban centres of Cyprus – Nicosia, Limassol, Larnaca and Fama-gusta – are in Mesaoria. Cyprus' international airport is based in Larnaca; Limassol and Famagusta are two deep-water harbours, frequented by hundreds of ships, and Nicosia is the seat of government, and the largest town on the island.

The **Northern Coastal Plain** is a narrow strip running from Cape Kormakitis eastward to Cape Andreas, between the Kyrenia Range and the sea. It is about 90 miles long, and no less than 3 miles wide. The island ends with the finger of

the Karpas Peninsula at the far east pointing into the sea.

The **Kyrenia Mountains**, or Besparmak (Mounts of the Five Fingers), separate the Coastal Plain from the Mesaoria Plain. The northern slopes of the mountains are covered with pine forests; the southern side is almost completely barren. The slopes of the Karpas Peninsula are a scrubland, rich with wild olive bushes; the soil is too thin and poor for anything but carob and olive trees. Along the beaches you may find some modest lemon and fruit groves.

Climate

Cyprus enjoys a very pleasant climate. However, July and August are rather hot, and may reach even 38°C (100°F), with

30°C (86°F) in the mountains. Nights are much cooler. In winter, the temperature seldom reaches 2°C (35°F), even in the mountains; in the coastal plains 4°-15°C (40°-60°F) and inland slightly less.

The average annual rainfall is 16 inches in the coastal plains, 12 inches inland, and 30 inches in the mountains; the rainy season – winter – lasts no longer than 80 days.

Seawater temperature ranges from 10°C (50°F) in winter to 27°C (80°F) in summer; water content is poor in salts and minerals, resulting in its vivid blue colour.

The People

Cyprus has a population of about 723,000, of which the majority are Greek (77%), with a Turkish minority of 18.4%. Another 4.5% are minorities such as Maronites, Armenians, Latins and others. The Greeks represent the original population of the island; the Turkish minority dates from the Ottoman rule (1571-1878), when the administration granted land confiscated from the original Greek owners to members of the Turkish garrison.

Regarding religious affiliation, 77% of the population are Christian Orthodox, 18% Moslem, and the rest are Catholic, Maron and Armenian Christians.

As soon as you leave the main roads, you will find yourself in another world: a few miles from the westernized modern towns, with their luxury hotels and high-rises, you will come across crumbling hamlets and isolated farms. Along the roads

Fruit picking in the groves surrounding Pafos

Agriculture still employs one third of Cyprus' economy

you will meet shepherds and labourers that seem to belong to times gone by.

The Languages

Greek is the main language of Cyprus, although Turkish is widely spoken. English is also widely spoken, as are French and German. There are several weeklies and one daily newspaper in English; day old copies of foreign dailies are

available at the main newsstands in all major cities. The local radio stations and the single TV channel broadcast daily programmes in English.

Learning Greek in Cyprus

Several modern institutes offer courses in spoken modern Greek. For information call the Ministry of Education in Nicosia, Tel. (02-303331). The American Centre (33B Leoforos Omirou, Nicosia, Tel. 02-473145) or the British Council (3 Odos Mouseiou, Nicosia, Tel. 02-442152), might also be able to assist you. For further details consult the CTO.

Economy

During the 60's Cyprus enjoyed a period of prosperity, which ended with the 1973 drought and the 1974 civil war. The ensuing partition disrupted all economic ties between the sectors. The Greek side was able to make a fast comeback; today there is practically no unemployment, and the financial situation is stable. The Turkish sector is still rather backward, with a high rate of unemployment and a very low standard of living. The information below refers to the economy of the Greek sector.

Agriculture employs one third of the labour force, and generate an income which amounts to 20% of the GNP.

Grain is widely grown (25% of the total agricultural output), mainly for local consumption; some of the other products are potatoes, grapes, citruses, vegetables and milk – mainly for export. Sheep farming is also

Tourism is a major source of income in Cyprus' economy

common, particularly in natural pastures on the hills.

Minerals were formerly Cyprus' main resource, although today they amount to very little: almost all the mines are in the northern, Turkish, zone; prices are low and the ore is poor.

Industry employs about 25% of the labour force, mainly in small private plants producing consumer goods and foodstuff, especially tobacco and wine for export.

Almost half the labour force is employed in **Public Services** – banks, transportation and tourism.

Tourism is Cyprus' major source of foreign currency. In 1994 tourists amounting to more than twice the island's population visited it, bringing in more than one billion US$. In fact, Cyprus, with its approx. 723,000 people, has ample facilities for four times as many tourists, with dozens of new hotels, sites and activities.

In spite of this, the economy of Cyprus is still in the red: it exports wine, potatoes, copper and citrus to Europe and imports raw materials, fuel, grain and consumer goods from Europe, the USA and Japan.

Byzantine and Gothic Architecture

Most churches and monasteries in Cyprus are in Byzantine or Gothic style.

During the Byzantine Era, starting with the 4th Century AD, even the smaller centres had their own basilica, with its characteristic elongated nave and atrium. Today, however, none of these remain.

What remains are shards of mosaic floors, the remnants of centuries of religious wars. Perhaps the most interesting is at Angeloktistos, a small village not far from Larnaca. This mosaic depicts the Virgin

The Byzantine structured tower of St. Lazarus Church in Larnaca

Mary holding the Infant in her arms, with two Archangels – Gabriel and Michael – at her sides. More about Cyprus' mosaics will be mentioned in the following chapters.

Other fragments have been recovered at Lambousa, near Kyrenia, in the Turkish zone, and are housed at the **Cyprus Museum** in Nicosia and in the British Museum, in London.

Glass artifacts in Lefkara

Five-domed basilicas, such as Agia Paraskevi in Geroskipou (near Pafos), are later structures developed from earlier, three-domed models such as those at **St. Barnabas** in New Salamis or **St. Lazarus** in Larnaca.

Later Byzantine structures are often decorated with fresco paintings, modelled on similar works of art common in 11th and 12th century Constantinople. Shards of such frescoes can be seen in St. Nicholas of Kakopetria and in the Asinoa Church (both high in the mountains) and in some other sites as well.

The Lusignan reign introduced Cyprus to the Gothic style. Gothic churches and cathedrals were built in Kyrenia, in Pyrga and in Famagusta. These were almost exact copies of contemporary churches in Northern France, home of the Lusignans. Later, during the 14th Century, the architects of Cyprus were inspired by Southern French churches. At the Moutoullas mountain church, which dates from the same period, the influence of oriental schools of religious art is evident in the frescoes.

From the beginning of the 15th century, Venice became the major influence, both in architectural structure and in interior decoration (see the Galata Church, 1502). The Gothic style, however, did not disappear from Cyprus. It is represented, for instance, in

16th and 17th Century buildings, such as Bedestan and St. Dhometios in Nicosia.

Arts and Crafts

The handicrafts of Cyprus have been famous for centuries, handed down from generation to generation. Precious stones, metal, wood or textiles, silk, wool and cotton, all are used to produce exquisite Cypriot craftsmanship. King Agamemnon received a splendid golden mail from Cyprus; Alexander the Great's famous sword also hailed from Cyprus. Cyprus' handicrafts can be admired at the National Museum and at the Folklore Museum of Nicosia (see "Nicosia").

Cyprus Handicraft Centres:
A large selection of handicrafts is available at the outlets of the *Handicraft Centres,* where you can also get guidance and information. There you will find Lefkara Lace, Kornus pottery, Phiti-type weaving and much more:

Nicosia: 186, Athalassa Ave., Tel. (02) 305024.
Larnaca: 6, Kosma Lysioti, St., Tel. (04) 630327.
Limassol: 25, Themidos St., Tel. (05) 330118.
Pafos: 64, Apostolou Pavlou, Tel. (06) 240243.

Souvenirs from all over Cyprus are available at the Handicraft Centre outlets

PART TWO – SETTING OUT

How to Get There

BY AIR

Several European and Middle Eastern Airlines connect Larnaca's Airport with most European Capitals: *Cyprus Airways* (CYP), 21 Odos Alkaiou, P.O.Box 1903, Nicosia, Tel. (02) 443054, fax (02) 465428. The booking office is at 50 Leoforos Archiepiskopou Makariou III, Nicosia, Tel. (02) 441996. Several weekly flights to Athens, Rome, Paris, London, Manchester, Birmingham, Munich, Zürich, Geneva and other cities are offered.

During the high season, dozens of additional charter flights connect Cyprus with Europe, and especially Great Britain, Germany and Scandinavia. Such flights often land at Pafos Airport, comfortably close to some of the best seaside resorts.

The following airlines have

A bus station in Pafos

their main branch in Nicosia: *British Airways*: 52A Leoforos Archiepiskopou Makariou, Nicosia, Tel. (02) 442188, fax (02) 446017.

Alitalia: 52 Leoforos Evegorou, Nicosia, Tel. (02) 464500, fax (02) 461894.

KLM: 24 Odos Th. Theodotou, Nicosia, Tel. (02) 443144, fax (02) 459497.

Lufthansa: Gonia Leoforou Arch. Makariou & Evagorou, Capital Centre, Nicosia, Tel. (02) 451777, fax (02) 366654.

Swissair: 6 Odos Pringkipissis de Tyras, Nicosia, Tel. (02) 445222, fax (02) 447222.

The Turkish zone (the Turkish Republic of Northern Cyprus) has no direct airway connections with Europe. From Ankara, Istanbul, Adana or Antalia (in Turkey) you can transfer to a local flight of the *Cyprus Turkish Airline* (*KTHY*), Tel. 441996. The London Office of *KTHY* is at Tel. 2415511; the Istanbul Office is at Tel. (212) 2465137.

BY SEA

Several shipping lines frequent Cyprus' main harbours, connecting the island with Italy, Greece, Israel, Lebanon,

Egypt, Syria, Turkey etc. Of course, if the flight-time to Cyprus, from Europe, is 4-5 hours at the most, a Mediterranean cruise may take over a week.

The seafares vary according to a very simple scale: you may travel on deck (for less than half the price of an airflight), or you may travel in a luxury stateroom, equal to a room in a five-star hotel – and pay accordingly.

Your travel agent will probably be able to inform you of all Mediterranean cruises and shipping lines, their timetables and their prices.

People of leisure may reach Cyprus by (hired or private) yacht. Cyprus has five Yachting Clubs: two in Larnaca, two in Limassol and one in Pafos. Often, on a single day, you can see over two hundred yachts moored at the Larnaca Marina – hailing from all the major European ports and even farther.

In the Turkish zone, a regular line connects Kyrenia with the port of Mersin (in south-eastern Turkey); both Kyrenia and Famagusta have adequate facilities for visiting yachts.

CROSSING THE LINE BETWEEN THE TWO ZONES
Tourists attempting to cross the line from Greek Cyprus to the Turkish zone should be prepared for all sorts of delays

At the main harbour of Limassol

and even abuse. The only crossing points are at the Nicosia gates; crossing in the opposite direction is simply out of the question.

Documents

Foreigners need a valid passport or other official documents confirming national identity in order to enter Cyprus as a tourist. Your travel agent will certainly know whether a visa is necessary and will be able to assist you in obtaining it. At the entrance gate, officials may inquire whether visitors possess sufficient funds to cover their stay (at least $30 per day).

For further information regarding passports and visas apply to the Migration Dept. in

Nicosia, Tel. (02) 303138, fax (02) 366944.

If you want to drive a vehicle in Cyprus, it is necessary to have on you an international driver's license with an identifying photograph attached to it. Your insurance should be issued by a company that is

Interesting and colourful Cypriot artifacts for sale

authorised to transact insurance business in Cyprus; otherwise it is possible to obtain insurance coverage when you arrive, at the ports of Limassol or Larnaca.

Health insurance is absolutely a "must"; insuring one's luggage against theft or loss is also highly recommended.

Customs

Cyprus laws exempt tourists from payment of customs for up to 250 grams tobacco; one litre of liquor, one bottle of wine and 0.30 litre of perfume.

You may bring in (and take out) up to 50 Cyprus pounds, and unlimited foreign currency. The laws state that sums exceeding $1,000 should be declared on entrance, but this law is not usually observed. You may bring in a vehicle and a boat - but you will not be allowed to hire them out or to sell them. The *Green Insurance Card*, valid in Europe, is not valid in Cyprus, but at most ports of entry you may purchase short term insurance policies for your vehicle and other effects.

For additional information contact the Nicosia Customs Authority, Tel. (02) 303175.

When to Come

The ideal seasons are spring and autumn, when temperatures are most comfortable, the weather is dry and the tourist resorts are seldom overcrowded. In the high season (July and August) you will be well advised to reserve your accommodation in advance. Most resorts and beaches will also be crowded.

Holidays

The following list includes general holidays as well as local festivals, religious and otherwise, held in various towns and villages.

1 January – New Year. House-wives bake a traditional loaf, called *Vasilopitta*, with a coin hidden inside it for good luck.

6 January – Epiphany. In the coastal towns, the priests throw a holy cross into the sea, and the most daring and coura-geous youngsters dive in to retrieve it.

24 January – St. Neophytos. Celebrated at the holy Neophy-tos Monastery at Pafos. Neophytos' tomb is decorated with beautiful frescoes. Hundreds of pilgrims flock to the monastery from all over the island.

2 February – Ypapante Day. Villagers pilgrimage to the Chrysoroyiatissa Monastery near Pafos, which, according to tradition, houses an icon representing St. Lucas the Apostle.

8 February – St. Theodoros, celebrated at Ktima and at Agios Theodoros.

10 February – St. Charalam-bos, celebrated at Dhenia, east of Nicosia.

9 March – Forty Martyrs' Day, celebrated at Yiolo, near Pafos.

25 March – Greek National

Practising religion at a church in Lefkara

Holiday and the Annunciation; special ceremonies are held at Klirou and Kalavassos.

1 April – Greek Cyprus Day.

6 April – St. Lazarus, patron of Larnaca.

23 April – St. George. Celebrated in many villages; a special ceremony is held at St. George's Monastery in Larnaca.

Religious ornamentation at the St. Lazarus Church in Larnaca

The entrance to the Stavrovouni Monastery

Good Friday and Easter Sunday (there is no fixed date).

1 May – Mayday. A national holiday. All businesses are closed.

50 days after Easter – Harvest festival; flower festival in Pafos.

26 July – Agias Paraskevi, celebrated in Nissou, Germasogia and Geroskipou.

15 August – The Dormition of the Virgin Mary, celebrated in all major monasteries: Kykkos, Chrysoroyiatissa, Troditissa and Machairas.

14 September – The Exaltation of the Holy Cross, celebrated at the Stavrovouni Monastery. On this day hundreds of faithful Christians join in prayer around a fragment of the holy cross, which according to an ancient tradition was brought from the Holy Land by St. Helena.

Last week of September – the Agia Napa festival.

1 October – Independence Day.

18 October – St. Lucas, celebrated in Nicosia, Evrihou, Kolossi and Palekori.

28 October – Greek National Holiday.

21 November – a fair and religious festival in Agros.

25 December – Christmas.

26 December – St. Stephan's Day – second day of Christmas.

How Long to Stay

You will need at least a week to go through the towns and villages, beaches and mountains of Greek Cyprus. Cyprus is a small island, and even the most conscientious tourist will cover his itinerary in less than two weeks. The Turkish zone, should you reach it, is even smaller.

How Much will It Cost?

Cyprus' very moderate prices are a good reason to visit. It is cheaper than most of Europe, and even cheaper than some other Middle Eastern countries. Five-star hotels and gourmet restaurants, however, are expensive in Cyprus. Car rental rates are actually high. Staple foods are very cheap, specially if bought at the marketplace. Public transport, theater, film tickets and other entertainment are also very affordable. Private lodgings are very expensive.

Wandering around Cyprus can be very cheap. Hitchhikers will probably manage with less than $70 a day for two ($25 for the night, $25 for food and $8-12 for transportation). Add ten percent for emergency expenses. More information is provided in the following chapters.

A more traditional tourist will opt for 2-3 star hotels ($50 for two), eat at modest restaurants ($35 for two daily – for breakfast and two full meals); as for transportation – this will cost about $10, or $40 with a rented car.

For the extravagant, $300 a day (for two) will be ample, including the hire of a comfortable car.

What to Wear

Good walking shoes, for informal sportswear, short-sleeved shirts and a sun-hat are necessary gear in summer; warm woollens and a good parka are needed in winter. Formal dress is required only at the most prestigious hotels. Wear what makes you feel comfortable.

If travelling by boat, bring your own sleeping bag and lots of woollens; at night the deck of a ship will be always very damp and often rather cold, even in the warmer seasons.

PART THREE – EASING THE SHOCK: WHERE HAVE WE LANDED?

Getting Around

Cyprus is small, and distances are short. Many of the roads are not very good. In the mountains, they are usually little more than a goat track. However, the condition of the roads gradually improves.

FINDING YOUR WAY AROUND

Street names are clearly indicated in all main towns both in Greek and in English. The original Greek names, however, are freely transliterated into English. This may cause occasional problems: your map mentions, for example "Lidras St.", but all you find at the street corner is "Ledra St";

"Pafos" can also appear as "Paphos".

In 1995 the Cypriot authorities initiated a policy aimed at unifying place names according to the original Greek. Thus Nicosia, the Capital, has become Lefkosia. The English names are marked in brackets.

Public Transportation

Buses are by far the most popular and convenient means of transportation. They will get you practically anywhere on the island – but they are rather slow, crowded, stuffy and obsolete. At most Tourist Offices (CTO) you will find a timetable of all major bus lines. Keep it handy: if you miss your bus, you may have to wait several hours for the next. Buses run from 5.30am to 7pm, but in the high season many lines run until midnight. Prices are surprisingly low.

There is also a **Shared Taxi Service**, more comfortable, faster but also more expensive. Buy your ticket and share a taxi with 4-6 other travellers. You may reserve your ticket by telephone, and the taxi will probably pick you up on time at your hotel. This service only runs between the main towns.

Shared taxis are run by *Kyrdas Inter Express*; for further details on the local offices – see the itinerary chapters.

There are also, of course, private taxis. They will take you anywhere on the map – for a price. They have a fixed tariff, valid between 6am and 11pm; in the early hours of the morning prices are hitched up by 15%.

HIRING A CAR

Following British tradition, motorized vehicles keep to the left side of the road. If you are used to right-side driving, take care.

All major international car rental agencies (such as *Europcar*, *Avis* and *Hertz*) operate in the island. Their prices are higher than those of local agencies, but their cars are generally more reliable. On the whole, car-hire prices are higher than in Western Europe.

Cars may be hired in one location and returned elsewhere; minimum hire is one full day, and the car has to be returned at the prescribed hour; failure to report on time will result in an additional fee. Most credit cards are accepted.

In the high season, the only way to find a car for hire is by advance reservation through your agent.

In most towns you will also be able to hire motorcycles and bicycles.

Hired vehicles, identified by a red licensed plate, are **not allowed** to cross from the Greek to the Turkish zone.

PRIVATE CARS

If you bring your car with you, you are allowed to use it freely during your stay; but if it is a standard model (left-hand drive) you will probably experience some unease driving on the left side of the street.

As we have already mentioned, road conditions are often quite rough. Many of the roads are two way, one or two lanes at most, and the farther you go from urban civilization, the higher the risk is of finding yourself travelling along what is called a "country road" on your map but is actually a goat track. To enjoy your driving in Cyprus, you have to be at least moderately adventurous.

Petrol stations are found on all the main roads. They are open at 6am-6pm (Saturdays until

Two-wheeled vehicles for hire

4pm). Some stations remain open throughout the weekend.

Traffic Regulations are standard, except for left-side driving. Children under 5 are forbidden to use the front seat. Distances are indicated in kilometres.

Maximum Speed is 50 k.p.h. in urban zones, 65 on inter-urban roads and 100 on the highway.

Parking is forbidden along pavements which are marked with double yellow lines. Single yellow lines allow limited parking, as indicated by sign.

The *Cyprus Automobile Association* (CAA), 12 Odos Chr. Mylona, P.O.Box 2279 Nicosia, Tel. (02) 313233, fax (02) 313842. It offers a range of services for the car owner, including discounts on air/ sea tickets, hotels, touring facilities, legal advice and breakdown emergency.

BICYCLES

Cyprus is a relatively small island, and most of the sites are within pedalling distance. Riding a bicycle on Cyprus' roads may however be rather dangerous; in the hilly regions, it is also very exhausting. For further information, call the *Cyprus Bicycle-riders Federation*, situated at Nicosia, 5 Visiinos St., Tel. (02) 456344. In the itinerary chapters you will find also some programmes suitable for bicycle riders.

Organized Tours

Several agencies offer a wide choice of organized tours. They will take you anywhere:

archaeological sites, churches and monasteries, quaint villages and nature reserves. Most of the tours are by coach; others by car, some by boat. There are also some sight-seeing programmes by night.

Regular programmes are morning-to-noon or morning-to-night. Overnight tours include a late dinner on site. Boat tours are offered from May to October. This includes pick up at your hotel, the services of a licensed guide and entrance tickets to sites and museums. Children under 12 pay half-price (not in restaurants). Further details at the CTO's and at most travel agencies.

Accommodation

There are hundreds of hotels, apartment hotels and registered pensions, ranging from luxury 5-star giants to single-starred hovels. There are also unregis-tered inns, pensions and youth hostels. The *Cyprus Tourist Organization* (CTO) publishes an almost complete list of hotels, including their classifi-cation, rating and services.

Hotel reservations can be made in advance through the *Cyprus Hotel Association* office situated at the Larnaca Interna-tional airport, Tel. (04) 643186.

At the apartment-hotels you may find studio apartments and 1-3 room suites. Apartment-

hotels are relatively cheaper than regular hotels.

Off-season prices are generally 50% lower than summer prices.

In summer it is advisable to reserve rooms in advance, at least in the more fashionable resorts; your travel agent may also find you some interesting bargains, cheaper than what you might find on arrival.

Five-star hotels provide their guests with the utmost luxury in all their services: air-condi-tioning, radio, TV sets, room telephone; swimming pools, bars, restaurants, nightclubs, saunas, tennis courts and other sport facilities. Often they will also offer baby-sitting services, medical care and services for the handicapped.

Four-star hotels provide their guests with high-standard

services, similar to their higher-priced competitors.

Three-star hotels are also comfortable and often as good as the higher class resorts.

Two-star hotels are clean and offer good accommodation, but their tourist services are considerably limited and more spartan.

Apartment hotels are classified in two classes – A and B. The services they provide include air-conditioned rooms, swimming-pools and a super-market.

Hotel prices may vary according to class, location and season; average double occupancy rates are as follows:
5 stars – $120-200
4 stars – $70-120
3 stars – $50-70
2 stars – $35-50
1 stars – $25-35

Apartment hotels:
Class A – $55-85 (room and kitchenette).
Class B – $35-55 (room and kitchenette).

Unclassified hotels are even cheaper.

There are **Youth Hostels** in Nicosia, Pafos, Troodos and Limassol; they cater only to members of the *IYHA* (International Youth Hostel Association). You may buy your IYHA membership at the Nicosia and Limassol Hostels.

Hostel prices range between $5-10 per night, including bed linen, blankets, service, taxes and breakfast. Showers are generally extra. For further details, apply to *The Cyprus Youth Association*, P.O.Box 1328 Nicosia, Cyprus, Tel. (02) 442027, fax (02) 442896.

Spindly palm trees grace the front of a hotel in Larnaca

Food and Restaurants

There are restaurants on almost every street corner, and in the major resorts, at almost every step. In summer, you will find most of them crowded with tourists. Off season, often the head waiter will stand at the door, trying to entice you to come in.

In comparison with European standards, restaurant prices are quite reasonable. Unquestionably, food will not be the highest item on your Cyprus budget.

Cypriot restaurateurs offer generally a single menu – take it or leave it. Exotic restaurants are still rare (although you will find several in Nicosia). Greek cuisine is the order of the day – but you will probably enjoy it.

Lunch is generally served 12am-2.30pm; dinner from 7.30pm onward. Restaurant prices are under the control of the CTO (Cyprus Tourism Office); they include a 10% service charge and a 3% CTO tax.

Cypriot cuisine is basically Greek, with Middle-Eastern nuances, such as the ever present *hummous*, *tahina* and *shishkebab*. Lemons are predominant, a true symbol of Greek cuisine.

Your menu will always begin

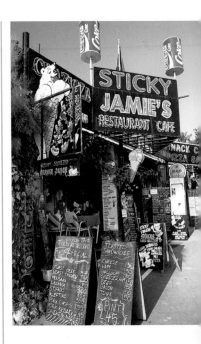

with a *meze* (or *mezedes*, or *mezedakia*). It will appear as a platoon of miniature dishes, with a foretaste of the entire menu. This will include the firsts courses – *hummous* (a chick peas paste, with paprika and olive oil), *tahina* (a sesame seed paste), *zaziki* (cucumbers in yogurt), village salad (tomatoes, cucumbers, olives with olive oil and goat cheese) and home-made *pitas* (flat breads).

For seconds you will have a choice of stuffed vegetables (*dolmades* – the most interesting is undoubtedly the stuffed vine-leaves – *koupepia*); *Haloumi* is firm goats-milk cheese, served grilled.

Then come the main servings: *sheftalia* (grilled minced pork),

39

moussaka (a slow-baked pie with eggplants, potatoes, minced meat, cheese and lots of spices), *stiffado* (a sort of stew redolent of onion), *afelia* (a pork stew in vine sauce), *tava* (baked lamb with onions) and *shishkebab* (pieces of mutton, small onions and tomatoes) – a dish that has already found its place in western menus.

Also very popular are *kleftiko Ofto* (lamb or goat wrapped in foil), *fasolada* (baked beans) and *zalatina* (smoked pork sausage).

There are, of course, fish restaurants as well, where you will find all sorts of deep sea fish, ink fish, octopus, shrimps and other delicacies.

For those who have a sweet tooth, there are several types of oriental sweets, like *souzoukko* (mashed nuts, almonds and other dry fruits in grapes and honey sauce), or *loucoumi* (known in Europe as Turkish Delight) – and a very sweet, very strong and very thick mini cup of coffee (if you like it unsweetened, be firm about it!).

If you're on a diet, you may order your own selection from the available menu, but do not be surprised if your bill is higher than that of those who ate the whole *meze*!

GLOSSARY
Arni – lamb
Elioti – olive bread
Feta – salty white cheese
Glyko – preserved fruits in syrup
Hirino – pork
Kalamari – squid
Kapari – pickled capers
Keftedes – meat balls
Kotopoulo – chicken
Loukanika – sausage

WINES
Wine is the pride of all Cyprus' farmers. Their vineyards produce some of the best wines in the world. The hills of Limassol and Pafos and the slopes of the Troodos Mountains are rightly known as some of the best vine-growing lands.

Cypriot wine was already famous at the time of the de Lusignan (13th and 14th Century). The three main wine-growing regions were (and still are) the Commandaria (near Limassol), Phoenix (near Pafos) and Templar (near Kyrenia). Some of the best Cyprus vines were introduced six centuries ago in the Champagne region (in France). Under the Ottoman rule the wine industry suffered a considerable setback, but it has since renewed its status.

A restaurant in Pafos

Today there are four major and very up-to-date wine-cellars (*Etko*, *Sodap*, *Loel*, *Keo*) and some minor, producers. Many are open to visitors, and you will be invited to view the wine-making process and to sample their wines.

Cypriots are not great wine consumers; they prefer brandy, rum and specially *ouzo* (an aniseed liquor).

The most famous of Cyprus' wines is undoubtedly the *Commandaria*. It is made from grapes grown on the Limassol hills. The harvested grapes are left in the open, to bake under the sun, for a fortnight before being processed by hand... and feet. The juice is kept until springtime, when it is brought to the cellars. There it will remain, in special oak barrels and at constant temperature, for ten years.

Keo is a pleasant local beer; the internationally famous *Carlsberg* has a plant in Cyprus too.

For further information or advice on Cypriot wine, you can contact the Ministry of Commerce and Industry, Tel. (02) 403441, fax (02) 366120.

Tourist Information

Tourism has been recognized by the government of Cyprus as the major financial resource of the island. Promotion of tourism has become one of the primary goals of the economy. And promotion of tourism means the creation of a wide range of tourist services of the highest possible standards. The CTO (*Cyprus Tourist Organization*) and its offices

The marina in Larnaca

offer their assistance for hotel reservations, cultural and entertainment programmes, guided tours, special events, timetables etc. As soon as you reach any town, check with the CTO desk, asking as many questions as you can think of and pick up any written material.

The head office of CTO is located at Nicosia. For information – P.O.Box 4535, CY 1390, Tel. (02) 337715, fax (02) 331644.

Licensed guides for touring in Cyprus can be contacted at the *Cyprus Tourist Guides Association*, P.O.Box 4942, CY 1355, Nicosia, Tel. (02) 457755, fax (02) 466872.

TOURIST INFORMATION OFFICES IN CYPRUS

Nicosia: 19 Leoforos Lemesou, Tel. (02) 315715.

Larnaca: Larnaca Airport, Tel. (04) 654389; Plateia Vasileos Pavlou, Tel. (04) 654322.

Limassol: 15 Spyrou Araouzou St., Tel. (05) 362756; Limassol Port, Tel. (05) 343868.

Pafos: 3 Gladstone St., Tel. (06) 232841.

Agia Napa: 17 Makarios Ave., Tel. (03) 721796.

Platres: Tel. (05) 421316 (April-October).

TOURIST INFORMATION OFFICES ABROAD

Britain: Cyprus Tourist Office, 213 Regent St., London, W1, R8-DA,Tel. (0171) 734-9822, fax (0171) 287-6534.

U.S.A.: Cyprus Tourism Organization, 13 E 40th St., New York, New York 10016, Tel. (212) 683-5280, fax (212) 683-5282.

Greece: Cyprus Tourist Organization, 36 Voukourestiou St., Athens 10673, Tel. (01) 361-0178, fax (01) 364-4798.

Italy: Ente Nazionale per il Turismo di Cipro, 6 via S. Sofia, Milano 20122, Tel. (02) 5830-3328, fax (02) 5830-3375.

France: Office du Tourisme de Chypre, 15 rue de la Paix, 75002, Paris, Tel. (01) 42.61.42.49, fax (01) 42.61.65.13.

For the Handicapped

The handicapped tourist will find a surprisingly wide network of services in Cyprus, beginning with landing assistance at the airport; special public transportation for wheelchair dependent tourists may be reserved through *Avis* (2 Homer St., P.O.Box 2276 Nicosia, Tel. 02-472062).

Many hotels are equipped for the provision of services for the handicapped; their list is available at the CTO offices. For further information, apply to *The Pancyprian Organization for the Disabled*, 50 Pendelis St., Dasoupolis, Nicosia, Tel. (02) 356767.

Sport

Water sports are extremely popular in all seaside resorts. Tourists may hire boats, water-skis and diving equipment at their hotel or at the water sport centres; weather information is available at the Coastal Meteorological Service (Tel. 04-630794).

Diving equipment is available at the Divers' Clubs of Pafos, Larnaca, Agia Napa and Limassol; for details call the Cyprus Federation of Underwater Activities (C.F.U.A) P.O.Box 1503, Nicosia, Tel. (02) 454647. Fishermen will find a guide to coastal fishing in Cyprus waters at the Fisheries Department of the Ministry of Agriculture, which is also useful to divers in their

underwater encounters with the local population.

Fishing is allowed only in specific reserves, and only to owners of a special permit; information, conditions and restrictions are available to tourists at the CTO's, or at the Department of Fisheries, 13 Odos Aiolou, C4 1101 Nicosia, Tel. (02) 303526, fax (02) 365955. Underwater fishing is forbidden.

Many hotels are equipped with tennis courts, and usually also offer tennis racquets for hire. For more information apply to Cyprus' Tennis Federation, P.O.Box 3931 Nicosia, fax (02) 458016.

Horse-riding is not a very widespread sport, and is considered a luxury: *Nicosia Riding Club*, P.O.Box 1783, Nicosia. Tel. (02) 379566.

Two golf courses operate on the island: *Tsada* Golf Club is situated north of Pafos, near the village of Tsada, Tel. (06) 642774/5, fax (06) 642776; *Elias* Golf Course is situated east of Limassol near Pereklisria village, Tel. (05) 325000, fax (05) 320880.The British military bases also maintain some good golf courses; a visit to the base as well as a game may be possible.

Soccer is the most popular grass roots sport, but its standards lag far behind those of European clubs.

September is the time of the Cyprus International Rally (car race). In winter (January and February), the ski runs of the Troodos are often open to the public. There are two runs for beginners (Sun Valley 1 and 2) and one for professionals (North Face).

Yachting is one of the more

popular sports on the island, thanks to excellent climatic conditions. Sailing boats or yachts can be hired at these facilities: *Orbit Marine Co.*, 122E Leoforos Lemesou, Nicosia, Tel. (02) 312901, fax (02) 426033; the *Old Salt Yachting Co.*, P.O.Box 7048 Limassol, Tel. (05) 337624, (05) 337768.

Shopping

Compulsive shoppers may find it difficult to satisfy their craving. Prices are not too high, but the choice is rather poor. Nicosia is the only place that can be rated as an adequate shopping turf.

Woolworth, *Marks and Spencer*, *Benetton* and *Stefanel* have local outlets in Nicosia.

Among local crafts, you will find outlets for the famous *Leftaritika* laces, hand-made jewels, silver *chanapias* (amphoras), copper objects, earthenware tools and wickerworks (see "Arts and Crafts").

General Information

Currency and Exchange

Cyprus' currency is the Cypriot pound (CYP), sub divided into 100 cents.

European currencies and US dollars are welcome everywhere, but you will find it easiest to change US dollars, British pounds and German marks. You may be asked to present your passport only when changing bank notes of $100 or travellers' cheques.

Credit Cards – *Master Card*, *Visa*, *Eurocard* etc. – are quickly taking their rightful place throughout Cyprus, specially in Nicosia and at the seaside resorts. Bank notes or travellers' cheques, however, are more welcome.

In the case of a lost credit card, you can contact the JCC Payment System Ltd. in Nicosia, Tel. (02) 365655.

Banks are open Monday-Friday, 8.30-12.30am (centrally located banks provide "afternoon tourist services" from Tuesday to Friday); in the afternoon you

may also change money at the Tourist Centres (3-5.30pm in winter and 4-6.30pm in summer). The airport money-changers at Larnaca and Pafos are open around-the-clock, even on Sunday; money-changers stay open very late also at the seaports.

Do not change all your money on arrival – but make sure you have enough local currency to last you over the weekend.

Working Hours

Most shops open their doors for business at 8am, close for a siesta at 1-4pm, and end their day at around 7pm. In winter their siesta is shortened to 2.30pm, and shops close at 5.30pm. Wednesday and Saturday afternoons most shops are closed.

Public services run a five-day week, 7.30am-2.30pm, on Thurs. also 3-6pm, and stay closed Saturday and Sunday.

Other offices open 8am-1pm and 4-7pm (in winter 2.30-5.30pm) and keep a five day week (closure on Saturday and Sunday).

Petrol stations are open 6am-6pm (Saturday only until 4pm); most of them do not open on Sunday.

Consular services are open Monday to Friday, 9.30-12.30am.

Posts and Telephones

In every town you will find at least one post office, open 7.30am-1.30pm, Thurs. 3-6pm (except July-Aug.) International-al trunk calls can be made directly from the Telephone Office and from many public phones; for international calls dial 00, followed by the code of the country you are calling.

Local calls on public phones cost 2 cents; inter-urban calls cost 10-20 cents. You will find many public phones equipped for the use of a *Telecard*; sold at post offices and at several kiosks for CYP 2, 5 and 10.

The area codes are:
Nicosia – 02; Larnaca – 04; Limassol – 05; Pafos and Polis – 06; Paralimni and Agia Napa – 03.

The Media

The *CBC* net (FM, 94.8) broadcasts news in several foreign languages (English,

German, French, Swedish and Arabic). The British military transmitter *BFBS* broadcasts in FM (89.4 for Nicosia and 99.6 for Larnaca). The *BBC* overseas programs and the *VOA* (Voice of America) are also available to English speaking listeners.

The local press is, of course, mainly in Greek. There are one English language daily – the *Cyprus Mail* – and two weeklies, the *Cyprus Weekly* and the *Middle East Economic Survey*.

Films and Theatres

Cinemas open daily at 7.30pm; on weekends they screen three daily shows: 3.30pm, 7.30pm and 9.45pm. Foreign films often have English subtitles, Greek films are never translated.

Tips

Tips are always welcome. As for the size of the tip, there are no clear rules. Bills generally include a 10% service charge; perhaps the best policy is to leave the small change as a tip. Waiters, drivers, barbers and porters do expect to be tipped. The normal porter tip is 50 cents per item – in 5-star hotels at least $2.

Health

In all Cyprus hospitals and major clinics doctors generally speak at least one European language.

The clinics open at 9am and close at 7pm, with a lunch break 1-3pm. Tourists with valid insurance policies can be reimbursed.

Chemist's keep to the regular trade timetable. The address of emergency chemists, which remain open around-the-clock, is available at Tel. 192 or, in Nicosia only, Tel. 1402. A list of overnight pharmacies is also listed in the daily newspapers.

During summer, beware of too much sun; sun-lotions are necessary for your protection – and they are on sale at every supermarket, perfumery and chemist's.

It is better to avoid drinking tap water; bottled mineral water is available everywhere.

It goes without saying that you should always carry a small first aid kit, with a few plasters and your favourite pain-killers.

Chronically ill and allergy-prone tourists will of course bring their medications with them. If you wear glasses, bring an extra pair, just in case.

Personal Security

Cyprus is a law-abiding country, with little if any violence in the streets, at any hour of the day and night. Even young women walking alone are seldom molested. Probably the highest risk one runs on the street is the sun...

If you drive, be careful. Cyprus' roads are sometimes inadequate, and left side driving may be a hazard, not only if you are a regular right-side driver, but also if – as is often the case – the driver you pass is a right-side driver.

Weights and Measures

Cyprus has recently joined the metric system, but old customs are hard to die:

1 pic – 61cm.
1 yard – 91.44cm.
1 oke – 1.28 kg.
1 gallon – 4.54 l.

Electric current is, like everywhere else in Europe, 220V; however, do not forget to check on the spot.

Local time is GMT +2.

A Suggested Tour in Cyprus

This book aims to provide the reader with a practical guide to the highlights of Cyprus. Our itineraries cover the entire island, in an easy-to-follow geographical sequence.

Your starting point will probably be Larnaca or Pafos international airports, or Limassol, if you are coming by sea. Visitors to the Turkish side will arrive at Kyrenia or Ercan (a small airport near Nicosia).

We will start out with Larnaca, proceed to Limassol and follow the coastline to Pafos. We shall then cross the Troodos Mountains to reach Nicosia. From here visitors may cross over to the Turkish zone, or turn to the coastal plain.

The length of your trip depends on your itinerary: you

Ruins of the Ylatis Sanctuary of Apollo

may wish to stop for a while on the mountains, or at one of the alluring beaches of Cyprus, or at some old monastery.

For those wishing to cross over to the Turkish zone, we have added a brief chapter on the northern shores of the island, as well as a sketch of Turkish Nicosia (see "Turkish Cyprus").

Agia Napa Bay

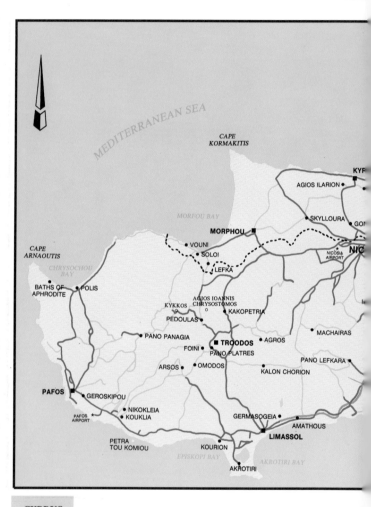

CYPRUS

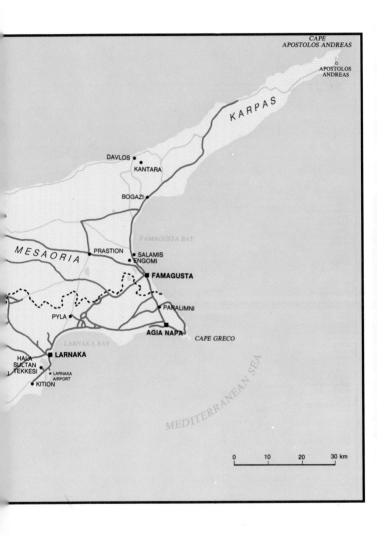

CYPRUS

LARNACA (LARNAKA)

Larnaca, the most modern of Cyprus' towns, is situated on the Nicosia-Limassol highway, and is just an hours' drive away from both Nicosia and Limassol. A few miles eastward, at Dhekelia, are some of the most attractive beaches in the Eastern Mediterranean, as well as dozens of modern luxury and apartment hotels. Larnaca itself has a population of 60,000 people.

Larnaca's former name was Kition or Kittim (one of Noah's descendants). The name Larnaca is derived from the Greek word *larnax* (coffin), probably a reminder of the many ancient coffins found on Kition's grounds.

Kition was one of the towns settled by the Mycaeneans in the 13th Century BC, which makes it the most ancient town in Cyprus. Under the Ottoman and British rule, Larnaca was the main trade centre of the island. At the beginning of our century it lost its rank, first to Famagusta (1918) and later to Limassol. Larnaca's seaport today seldom sees large ships – but it still caters to hundreds of private yachts. It has several industrial plants, as well as a large oil refinery. Larnaca is slowly rebuilding its overseas trade now, along with Famagusta in the Turkish zone.

The Larnaca Marina

How to Get There

By Air: The Larnaca International Airport (Tel. 654389) is situated less than 2 miles from the town centre. A taxi service connects the airport with the centre of town; The No. 21 bus line also commutes from town to the airport – on average of once an hour. The last bus leaves at 5.30pm in winter, at 7pm in summer, and at 1pm on Saturday. There is no bus service on Sundays.

By Sea: Shipping lines do not use the port of Larnaca, apart from an occasional cruise-boat. The yacht marina, on the other side is one of the largest and most frequented by European and Middle Eastern yachtsmen.

Larnaca may also be reached by *water-taxi* from Agia Napa. The crossing takes an hour and sails from Agia Napa's fishermen's pier to the Larnaca Marina. A timetable is available at Captain George's, on the marina pier (Tel. 653110).

By Land: Larnaca's bus terminal extends along the whole length of Leoforos Athinon Ave., the town's main promenade, alongside the marina. It serves as a terminal for the Nicosia, Limassol, Pafos, Agia Napa and Troodos bus lines. The airport bus stops in front of the *Sun Hall* Hotel. The *Kallenos* Company buses leave for Nicosia once an hour from 5.45am to 4.45pm, and for Limassol every two hours, also from 5.45am to 4.45pm.

For more information call Tel. 654890. Don't expect Swiss precision, however!

The *E.M.A.N* Company (Tel. 03-721321) handles the Agia Napa line, with hourly buses in summer (every two hours in winter).

Makris' Shared taxis coming from Nicosia and Limassol stop at Sileos Paveou St., not far from the marina.

Tourist Services

Larnaca's CTO (Cyprus Tourist Organization) is situated at the marina entrance, at the northern end of Athinon Ave. (Tel. 654322). Here you will find a map of Larnaca, information flyers and a timetable of the urban bus network. Another CTO office located at the airport is open around-the-clock. At the airport you will also find 24-hour bank services and a flight information desk. The CTO will be glad to assist you with hotel reservations and guided tours. Cyprus Airways also has an office at the airport.

CYPRUS

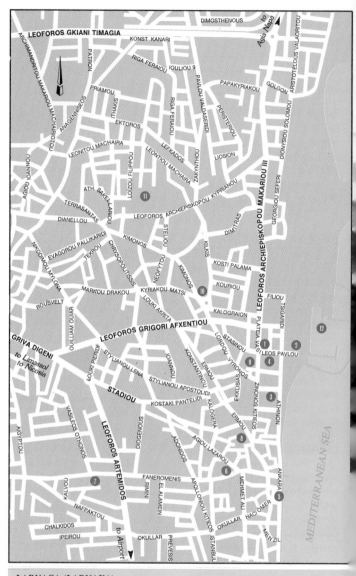

LARNACA (LARNAKA)

1. CTO Office
2. E.M.A.N. Terminal
3. Kallenos Terminal
4. Makris Taxi Service
5. Larnaca Castle
6. St. Lazarus Church
7. Agia Phaneromeni Church
8. Larnaca Market
9. Pierides Foundation Museum
10. Larnaca Archaeological Museum
11. Ancient Kition's Acropolis
12. Marina

All major Cyprus banks have branches in Larnaca. You will find most of them on Zinons Kitieos St. (the main shopping centre) and further north, on Makarios III Ave. The *Bank of Cyprus*, at 25 King Paul Sq., Tel. 623181, is open to tourists also in the afternoon.

Larnaca's post office is also located on Zinonos Kitieos, north of the Sileos Pavlou corner.

Telegrams can be sent by phone Mon.-Sat., from 7am to 7pm, by dialling 196. On Sundays and holidays telegrams are only accepted at the *Cyprus Telecommunications Authority* on Lord Byron St.

The Telephone Office is on Lordou Vyronos St., also not far from the shopping centre.

Urban Transportation

The streets are not too crowded, and are pleasant to drive along in a car or bike; however, there are few parking facilities. The buses are cheap but outdated; and, of course, there are many private taxis.

CAR HIRE

Most car-hire agencies have branches in Larnaca. Some local firms have their only base in Larnaca. At the airport you will find *Hertz, Avis, Europcar* and the large local

On the promenade at Larnaca

firm of *A. Petsas*. All four also have downtown branches:

Europcar: Artemidos Ave., 7-8 Joanna Court, Tel. 657442, 657462.

Hertz: 33F Makarios III Ave., Tel. 655145; at the airport, Tel. 622388.

A. Petsas: Gr. Afxentiou Ave., Carithers Ct., Tel. 623033; at the airport, Tel. 657850.

Avis: 43 Makarios III Ave., Tel. 657132; at the airport, Tel. 657920.

Accommodation

There is a wide choice of hotels and apartment hotels. The downtown hotels are suitable for shorter stays, and are also somewhat cheaper. The hotels on the north-eastern beach strip are of the sea resort type, well equipped with entertainment and sport facilities and medical assistance; they are generally very modern and rather more expensive.

5-STAR HOTELS

Golden Bay: Larnaca-Dhekelia Rd., Tel. 645444, fax 645451. Far from the town centre, along the coastal road to Agia Napa. A true luxury resort, with a wide selection of services.

4-STAR HOTELS

Palm Beach: Larnaca Dhekelia Rd., Tel. 644500, fax 644770. Larnaca's best 4-star hotel, with 5-star services (TV in the room is an extra!); no services for the handicapped; on the beach.

Sandy Beach: Larnaca Dhekelia Rd., Tel. 646339, fax 646900; on the beach. Outdoor swimming pool.

Sun Hall: Athinon Ave., Tel. 653341, fax 652717. Very central; no private beach.

3-STAR HOTELS

Beau Rivage: Larnaca Dhekelia Rd., Tel. 623600. On the strip, with private beach.

Flamingo Beach: Pyiale Pasa, Tel. 650621, fax 656732. South of the town centre; no private beach; nice swimming pool; reasonably priced.

Four Lanterns: 19 Athinon Ave., Tel. 652011, fax 626012. Central; no beach and no pool.

2-STAR HOTELS

Arion: 26 Galileo St., Tel. 650200, fax 654253. Small cozy hotel, conveniently located, close to the centre of town and the shopping centre; swimming pool.

Les Palmiers Sun Hotel: on the corner of Athinon Ave. and Pieridou St., Tel. 627200. Air-conditioned rooms; no beach and no pool.

Eva: Larnaca Dhekelia Rd.,

Tel. 624100. On the north-eastern strip; some air-conditioned rooms; swimming pool.

I.B. Sandbeach Hotel: Piyale Pesa, Tel. 655437. Pleasant beach; no air-conditioning. On the southern strip.

INEXPENSIVE HOTELS
Pavion: 11 St. Lazarus Sq., Tel. 656688. Central, with some air-conditioned rooms. Open only during the high season: best to inquire!

The Rainbow Hill: 140 Zinons Kitieos, Tel. 621990. Near St. Lazarus Sq.; simple and cheap.

APARTMENT HOTELS
Sunflower: 69 Makarios III Ave., Tel. 650111. A Class. No beach, no pool, on the Larnaca-Agia Napa road. Studio apartments and 1-2 room suites.

Acropolis: corner of Ermou St. and Grigori Afxentiou Ave., Tel. 623700. B Class, central; studio apts. and 1-3 room suites; air-conditioned; swimming pool.

Athene Beach: 80 Athinon Ave., on the mall, Tel. 656272. B Class, central; studio apts. and 1-2 room suites; air-conditioned.

Adonis Beach: Piyale Pasa, Tel. 656644. B Class, far south of the town; no beach, no pool; air-conditioned.

Boronia: Larnaca-Dhekelia Rd., Tel. 646200. On the eastern strip; swimming pool; only one-room suites.

YOUTH HOSTEL
Larnaca's youth hostel is situated at 27 Odos Nikolaou Roussou, Tel. 621188.

CAMPING
The Camping site is 5 miles east of Larnaca, on the beach, in an eucalyptus grove, on the way to Agia Napa. Showers, toilets, minimarket and restaurant; tents for hire; electrical sockets. Tel. 644511.

Restaurants

Along the Athinou Ave. shopping arcade you will find dozens of restaurants, fixed menus and prices; no need to reserve tables.

Yin Yang Chinese restaurant: On the Larnaca-Agia Napa Road, along Palm Beach, on 19-24 Athens St., Tel. 652011.

Megalos Pefkos: A seafood

A restaurant in Larnaca, its front adorned with ceramic statuettes

restaurant, situated at the foot of the castle, on the beach. Tel. 628566.

Alasio: Larnaca-Dhekelia Rd., Tel. 645038. International cuisine, live band every Saturday.

Café Retro: 7 Afxentiou Ave., a pleasant downtown snack-bar and coffee house. Tel. 656268.

Shopping

In the past the Romans used to call Larnaca "Commercio", because the town was a major trading centre. Today Larnaca still offers its visitors a great variety of goods, such as jewellry, leather and the famous lace.

The main shopping areas are Hermes, Zinonos Kitieos and Grigoris Afxentiou – three very narrow streets, with lots of large modern shops and tra-ditional boutiques; mostly clothes and footwear, less home appliances and electronics.

Super Athienitis, on Gen. Timayia Ave., is a four-floor department store full of the best of everything: food and beverages, books and souvenirs.

Shae's is a leather shop and factory with garments made-to-measure, all at factory prices, 50 Lord Byron St., Tel. 04-654198.

Night life

Larnaca's night-life is not very hectic. "Late" (8-9pm) hour entertainment is limited to a leisurely walk along the promenade, or sitting at one of the promenade's many cafés and restaurants.

Disco fans can dance at the

Stringfellows Disco in Dhekelia Rd. Tel. 624157 – or at Cloud 9, on the seafront.

There are also a few Greek music spots on General Timagia St., and Makarios III Ave.

At the marina entrance you will find the *Marina Pub*.

Sports

The *Larnaca Tennis Club* – with its six tennis courts – is at 10 Kilkis St., Tel. 656999.

The Ochtabos Diving Centre, Tel. 650266, offers diving lessons.

At the Tourist Beach of Larnaca you will find water sport facilities.

FESTIVALS

February 18-28 – fancy dress parades and festivities in front of the town hall.

April 11 – procession of St. Lazarus, from St. Lazarus Church, in the evening.

June 7 – Festival of the Flood celebrations.

July – Larnaca festival.

November – fine arts month. Cultural events in the town hall.

Useful Phone Numbers

Larnaca area code: 04.
First Aid, Police, Fire Brigade: Tel. 199.
Hospital: Tel. 630300.
Flight Information: Tel. 654389 (24-hour).
Cyprus Airways: Tel. 654294.
Lost Property: Tel. 630200.
Self service laundromat: 5 Leoforos Artemidos, Tel. 624052.
CTO at Plateia Vasileos

Pavlou, Tel. 654322; CTO at the Larnaca International airport (a 24-hour service), Tel. 643000.

Larnaca Town Hall: Leoforos Athinon and Filiou Zannetou Sts., Tel. 653333.

Sites to See

Familiarize yourself with a few key points on the town map, starting with the beach strip, from Athinon Ave. southward along Ankara St. and Piyale Pasa. At the northern end of this promenade, you will find the marina. Parallel to the beach runs the Zinonos Kitieos shopping arcade, extending northward on Makarios III Ave., toward the Agia Napa Road. Lordou Vyronos (Lord Byron) St. and Kimonos St., branch off from Zinonos Kitieos towards ancient Kition and the suburbs.

Our itinerary begins at **Larnaca Castle** on Ankara St., along the beach. The castle was built in 1625 and originally served as a prison. From its promenade walls, enjoy a view of the Scala Quarter with its Büyük Kebir Mosque – formerly one of Larnaca's Turkish neighbourhoods. Today the castle houses an impressive archaeological museum, built like a labyrinth, and dedicated to ancient Kition and later periods. Open Mon.-Fri., 7.30am-2.30pm, Thurs. 3-6pm

On Larnaca's peaceful promenade

(no afternoon during July-Aug.), Tel. 630169, entrance fee.

From the castle, continue north along Ankara St. and turn left on Dionysus until you reach the corner of Faneromenis and Agiou Lazarou; on the corner is the **St. Lazarus Church** (Agiou Lazarou), built in the 9th century by Emperor Leo, on the site of St. Lazarus' tomb, in honour of the town's Patron Saint. According to legend, Lazarus travelled to Larnaca after his resurrection, and became the city's first bishop. His tomb is inside the church, under the main altar. The entrance is decorated with a number of icons; one of them depicts Lazarus' resurrection. The church belltower was built in 1857.

At the St. Lazarus Church, built on the site of St. Lazarus' tomb

The church also houses a small museum, containing beautiful samples of Byzantine religious art, including old wood carvings, icons and utensils.

Further, along Leoforos Phaneromenis is the **Agia Phaneromeni Church**, built above an ancient cave in the 8th century.

Return to St. Lazarus Church, and turn left along Ermou St. After a short walk, you will reach the **Larnaca Market**; Zinonos Kitieos St. should be on your right. This is one of the main shopping areas of Larnaca. Walk along it, enjoying the colourful shop-windows.

Beyond Lordou Vyronos St. (more about it later on), stands the **Pierides Foundation Museum**, with an imposing private archaeological collection, founded 1840 and later donated to the city. The museum is open Mon.-Sat., 9am-1pm; entrance fee, Tel. 651345.

Proceed to Lordou Vyronos St., and follow it north-westward until it crosses Grigori Afxentiou Ave. Continue westward along Grigori Afxentiou Ave. towards Larnaca's beautiful municipal park with the Museum of Natural History and a marble bust of the philosopher Zeno; or continue northward to Kimonos St., to the **Larnaca Archaeological Museum**, located near the Sisters' School of St. Joseph's (1844). In the museum several Neolithic and Bronze Age objects are exhibited, recovered in local digs. Open June-August, Mon.-Sat., 7.30am-1.30pm – and the rest of the year Mon.-Fri., 7.30am-2pm; Saturdays only until 1pm. Entrance fee, Tel. 630169.

About 300 yards past Kimonos, you will reach the **acropolis of ancient Kition**, which was for a time the capital of the whole island. Little remains of the ancient city, once rich in temples and palaces: all that remains are a few remnants of Heracles' and Aphrodite's temples, and several gold, bronze and ivory tombs of the 13th century BC.

Proceed to Archiepiskopou Kyprianou Ave.; at the corner you will see the 19th century Krissopolitissa Church. Turn right, to the **Kition Archaeological Site**. Archaeological digs have shown that Kition was founded by Mycenean traders in the 13th century BC, destroyed toward the end of that century and rebuilt by a new wave of Aegean immigrants. The Phoenicians conquered the town in the late 9th century BC, and from here tried to invade the inland. The Phoenicians held the town for three centuries, only to surrender it to Ptolemy I of Egypt (295 BC). The site is open Monday-Friday, 7.30am-

2:30pm; Thursday 3-6pm, no afternoon in July and August. Entrance fee.

This is the most important of the archaeological sites, where no fewer than five temples of the 13th and 12th century BC were unearthed, along with traces of a number of other structures. The first walls of Kition, made of enormous boulders, date from that period.

At the marina in Larnaca

Continue along Kilkis St., and turn left on Makarios III Ave. From there, turn right into Sileos Pavlou St. and to the **marina**, where there is a CTO office. Several small yachts, and other boats offering coastal tours as far as Famagusta, moor at the marina pier. For detailed information, call Captain George, Tel. 653110.

End with a leisurely walk southward, along the seaside promenade, with its quaint but attractive restaurants and bars.

The Salt Lake

Depart town along the airport access road; you will soon come across the **Larnaca Salt Lake**. This lake, which in winter is full and frequented by flamingoes, dries up by the end of July, leaving a 2-3 inch thick crust of salt. The lake, once connected to the sea, was apparently artificially transformed into a salt-water basin, to be duly harvested in the late summer months.

According to a legend, the salt lake was formed when a local woman refused Lazarus a bunch of grapes from her vineyard; the affronted Saint cursed the offender,

Larnaca's Salt Lake

changing her vineyard into a barren salt lake.

The truth is, of course, quite less dramatic. The area used to be a shallow, and particularly the salty lagoon, which dried up in summer. Its salt has been harvested since ancient times; later on, it was artificially closed off and turned into a "lake" at a time when salt was a mineral so precious, that the Roman soldiers' wages were often paid in salt: the term *salary*, in fact, derives from the latin word *salis* (salt).

Between the 12th and 14th centuries AD Larnaca was a very important seaport, and salt was its main commodity. Today salt harvesting is state run, but only for local consumption.

The harvest is done in part manually and in part by specially equipped small tractors. The salt is transferred to trucks for transportation to the packing plants. The lake is open daily; 1st June-30th Sep. 07:30am-7:30pm; from 1st Oct.-31st May 7:30am till sunset. Entrance free.

THE HALA SULTAN TEKKE MOSQUE

This Moslem shrine is located on the western shore of the Salt Lake. It was built in 1816, on the site of Umm Haram's Tomb. According to tradition, Umm Haram, Mohammed's foster mother, died here of a broken neck, having fallen from her donkey during one of the Moslem raids in 647. The Mosque is open to visitors June-September, 7.30am-7.30pm (Between Oct.-May until 5pm). Entrance free.

The Angeloktistos Church

On the same road, about 7 miles from Larnaca, is the village of Kiti (or Kition), with the **Panagia Angeloktistos**, an imposing 11th century Byzantine structure, with a later (14th century) Gothic front. Embedded in the floor is a 6th century mosaic depicting the Virgin Mary with the infant in her arms and the Archangels Michael and Gabriel at her sides; on the walls are icons from various periods.

Pyla

Leave Larnaca via Agia Napa. Turn left, less than four miles out of Larnaca, along the gulf, not far from the *Palm Beach Hotel*, and proceed about one mile, to the village of **Pyla**.

Until 1974 this was a mixed Greek-Turkish

settlement. Pyla is located within the territory of Greek Cyprus, but since it stands on the area of the British Dhekelia Base, it has become a joint Turkish-Greek enclave, policed by a United Nations contingent.

Pyla's church and its belltower date from the Middle Ages.

The Beaches

The Larnaca Tourist beach is administered by the CTO. It is a 6 mile strip running toward Agia Napa, and is equipped with dressing rooms, showers, beach-chairs, snack-bars and restaurants.

Sunbathing at a Larnaca beach

AGIA NAPA

Agia Napa is known throughout Europe as a famous tourist resort. It is one of Cyprus' most popular resorts, particularly among German and Scandinavian tourists.

The Golden Sands Beach in Agia Napa

This little village has less than 1000 inhabitants, but thanks to its unique location and splendid beaches, it hosts 10-15 thousand tourists daily, during the summer season! The beaches are strips of soft, thin sand, hidden among a chain of rocky boulders that form many small, cosy bays. In summer, the entire population of Agia Napa become workers at hotels, restaurants, supermarkets, discos, car-hire and bicycle agencies. There are also lots of gift-shops and other shops selling footwear, clothes and whatever one might need to buy.

The village owes its name, according to tradition, to a hunting party wandering in the forest, which came across an ancient cave with a splendid icon inside it. Hence "Napa" (forest) and "Agia" (saint) became Agia Napa (The Forest Lady Saint).

The main centre of the district is Paralimni, 3 miles north of Agia Napa itself. East of the village is Protaras, which has also become a tourist resort.

How to Get There

By Bus: There is an hourly minibus service that regularly (on the hour) commutes between the *Sun Hall Hotel* in Larnaca and the CTO Office in Agia Napa and vice versa.

Those coming from elsewhere on the island will have to stop over in Larnaca on their way to

Agia Napa; in the summer, however, there is a daily direct bus, leaving Nicosia (at Solomos Sq.) in the morning and returning in the late after-noon. Inquire (in Nicosia) at Tel. (02) 473414.

By Sea: *Water Taxi* from the Larnaca marina, Tel. 635405.

AGIA NAPA

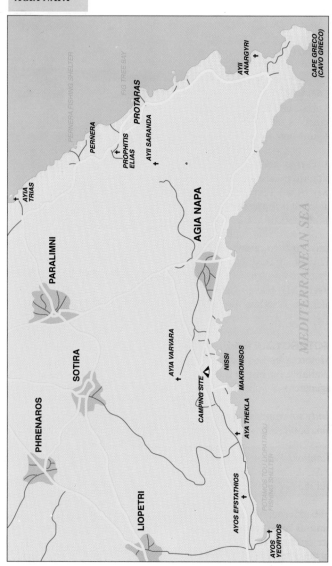

Tourist Services

The CTO Office is on Arch. Makarios Ave., Tel. 721796. Here you will find information on the district's hotels and beaches, which are in Agia Napa, Paralimni and Protaras, as well as good maps of the whole district. The CTO will also assist you with hotel reservations.

CAR HIRE
Almost all the major car-hire agencies are represented in Agia Napa:

A. Petsas: halfway between the monastery and the *Grecian Bay Hotel*, Tel. 721260. (*Budget* is represented by *A. Petsas*).

Avis: right in centre, Tel. 721844.

Hertz: Misiauli Kavazoglou St., Tel. 721836.

MOTORCYCLE HIRE
Motorcycles and bicycles are available for hire at these local agencies:

Andy's Panayi: 46 Stadium St., Tel. 650850.

Yiannaki Petros: Philyra St., P.A., Antoniou Bldg., Shop 1, Tel. 638765.

The village has branches of several banks, most of them are open for money changing in the afternoon. The main

branch of the *Cyprus Bank* is at 25 King Paul Sq., Tel. 623181.

The post office is near the monastery. To reach it, walk north, and turn right after the *Bank of Cyprus* branch.

Accommodation

In the high season it is very important to book rooms ahead of your visit. It is best to make your reservation through your local travel agent, who will provide ample information on hotels in the district . Should you find yourself in Agia Napa without accommodation, try to enquire at the local CTO; they will surely be glad to help you.

At the Grecian Beach, the Sandy Beach and the Nissi Beach there are clusters of hotels and apartment hotels. In Protaras and Paralimni there

A hotel in Agia Napa

are also several hotels and apartment hotels.

5-STAR HOTELS
Grecian Bay Hotel: little more than half a mile from the village, with its own private beach, Tel. 832000. The peak of local luxury – and, in season, the peak of Cyprus prices. Swimming pools, tennis courts, disco, sauna, *Bank of Cyprus* branch. Everything you need is on the hotel grounds.

4-STAR HOTELS
Grecian Sands: a little beyond the *Grecian Bay*, on the way to Protaras (Tel. 721616). Private beach and pools, tennis courts, disco; not less attractive, while substantially cheaper than the *Grecian Bay*.

Nissi Beach: About 1.5 miles west of Agia Napa, Tel. 721444. A little far from the village's hectic night life, but it has beach, pool, tennis, sauna and diving club.

Florida: Between the *Grecian Bay* and the *Grecian Sand*, but across the road, Tel. 721821. Very reasonable prices, but no private beach. A small hotel, with a small pool, tennis courts and sauna.

3-STAR HOTELS
Bella Napa Bay: Tel. 721601. East of the village; no private beach, but with a pleasant swimming pool and good tennis courts.

Sunwing: Kryou Nerou Ave., Tel. 723000. Private beach, swimming pool and tennis courts, and this is reflected in the prices. Less than one mile east of the village.

INEXPENSIVE HOTELS
1 and 2-star hotels are less comfortable; the following, however, may be pleasant enough for a short stay:

Chrysland: 2 stars, Tel. 721311. West of the village, no beach.

Leros: 1 stars, Tel. 721126. Very close to the village, on the road to the fishermen's pier.

APARTMENT HOTELS
Those willing to do without the luxuries of hotel lobbies, room and restaurant service, twice daily change of bedclothes and towels, can save money by staying at one of the resort's apartment hotels. The rooms are spacious and pleasant, and most of them are modern, con-

veniently located and equipped with swimming pools.

Anesis: A Class, modern, close to the village and to the Golden Sands Beach, Tel. 721104. 1-2 room suites, with modern kitchens and a pleasant sitting room. A small pool, snack-bar, bar, and a TV room.

Anthea: A Class, just south of the monastery, on the road to Larnaca, Tel. 721411. Two floors, with 84 suites with sitting room, bedroom, terrace, kitchen and showers; heated and air-conditioned; snack-bar, restaurant, pool and supermarket.

Limanaki Beach: A Class, at the fishermen's pier, south of the village, very close to the Golden Sands Beach. Tel. 721600. Studios and 1 room suites, with terrace, kitchen, sitting area, toilets and bathroom or shower. Snack-bar, pool and TV room. Air-conditioned.

Napa Prince: A Class. On the west side of Agia Napa, five minutes from the centre and half a kilometre from the sea. All the facilities that are mentioned above. Tel. 721483.

All four A Class hotels are reasonably priced. Others are slightly cheaper. A Class apartment hotels, can be found further away, west of the village at *Nissiana*, Tel. 721224 (not far from the Nissi Beach), or eastward at *Kermia Beach*, Tel. 721401.

Adams Beach: B Class. On the Nissi Beach, 1.5 mile from the village. Excellent range of services: private beach, pool and tennis courts, Tel. 721275.

Antia Maria: B Class. Central, near the CTO. Inexpensive, but no pool. Very close to the beach, Tel. 721921.

Castalia: B Class. On the west side of the village. Restaurant, supermarket, shopping arcade. With 78 1-3 room suites, all air-conditioned and fully equipped. Walking distance from the Sandy Beach. Swimming pool, restaurant and TV room. Next door to a bicycle and motorbike hiring agency, Tel. 721108.

Freminore: B Class. Near the *Castalia*; same services and prices. Small swimming pool; next door to supermarket, Tel. 721711.

Cornelia: B Class. Near the CTO. Small, inexpensive, but no pool; 1-2 room suites, Tel. 721406.

Eleana: B Class. Between the village and the Golden Sands Beach. One room suites only, with a bed corner in the sitting room. The hotel is fully equipped, and has air-conditioning, bar, snackbar, pool, TV room and mini market, Tel. 721640.

CAMPING

The camping grounds are situated 2km west of Agia Napa, on the right hand side of the road, a few meters from the sea. (Tel. 721946). Showers, toilets, mini market, bar, tents for hire and electrical sockets. Open from March to October.

Restaurants

Along the two main streets of the village – Leoforos Makariou and Agias Mavris – are scores of restaurants serving local cuisine, all similarly priced. The monastery side is crowded, but the upper end of Agias Mavris is quiet and attractive.

Shopping

Agia Napa is only a small village, but it has some very good shops along Makariou, Kryou Nerou and Eleftherias Sts., among them are gift shops, footwear, clothing and electronics.

Night life

Agia Napa is mainly a youthful resort, and the night life here is obviously louder and longer than anywhere else in the island. The *Majestic* discotheque is located within the *Karousos* Apartment Hotel, at the western end of Agia Napa. Tel. 722690; *VIP* is a restaurant with disco, across the street from the Tourist Information (CTO) office. Tel. 721540.

Sports

Sun Fish Diving Centre: 26 Makarios Ave., Tel. 721300.

Trum Diving Centre: at the *Capo Bay Hotel*, Paralimni, Tel. 822101.

Useful Phone Numbers

Agia Napa area code: 03
First Aid, Police, Fire Brigade: Tel. 199.
Police Station: Tel. 721553.
Port Police: Tel. 723322.
Cyprus Airways : Arch. Makarios Ave., Tel. 721265.
E.M.A.N. Buses: 32 Arch. Makarios Ave., Tel. 722190.
E.M.A.N Taxis: 1 A. Loucas St., Tel. 721379.
Bank of Cyprus: 7 D. Solomos St. Tel. 721470.
Post Office (with fax service): 13a D. Solomos St., Tel. 722141.
CTO: Arch. Makarios Ave., Tel. 721796.

Sites to See

The only historical site in the village of Agia Napa is the **Monastery** – one of the last palaces built by the Venetians before they lost the island in 1570. It was here, according to tradition, that the icon which gave the village its name was found.

The entrance gate and gate-house are characteristic of Venetian architecture. The monastery's water supply is provided by a Roman style aqueduct, ending in two cisterns. In the inner court you can find a curious pig-shaped water-fountain.

Agia Napa Monastery

The monastery was built in order to serve the local Catholic community. Later it was impounded by the Greek-Orthodox Church. In 1974 it became a shelter for displaced Greek refugees fleeing from the Turkish sector, and specially from Famagusta. A new wing, added in 1978, serves as a hostel and a multi-faith religious centre. Mass services take place at the following times: German Mass: 10am; Anglican Mass: 11am; Roman Catholic Mass: 5pm; Swedish Mass: 6pm.

Toward the end of September, the monastery hosts an annual three-day festival, with art exhibitions, entertainment and various shows.

The Agia Napa District

PROTARAS AND PARALIMNI

A visit to Protaras and Paralimni is a must. It is a very pleasant 20 mile trip by motor-cycle or bicycle.

Start toward the south-eastern end of the

island, **Cape Greco**. Near the promontory, where the roads snakes northward, turn right onto a narrow lane climbing to the promontory itself, with its impressive boulders and ridges. Back to the main road, proceed northward for about 3 miles to Protaras, a small village, quickly becoming a tourist resort.

Follow the road northward; turn right to visit the **Agios Trias Church**, high on the beach. The road continues on to the border with the Turkish Zone, 2 miles further on, towards Famagusta. Turn left to Paralimni.

PARALIMNI

Paralimni is the largest centre in the district. Its CTO is open from July to September. The Paralimni Church is called **Agios Georgiou**.

From Paralimni turn back southward to Agia Napa.

A WALK TO PARALIMNI

Agios Georgiou Church in Paralimni

A 9 mile walk will take you to Cape Greco and to Protaras. If you get tired along the way, the buses can always be flagged down from the roadside.

Start from Agia Napa along the main road to Protaras. After less than a mile, where the road turns northward near the *Sunwing Hotel*, leave the road and follow the path that runs along sand beaches and rocky boulders toward Cape Greco. Don't walk barefoot!

Approaching the Cape, you will see a small lighthouse and the towering aerials used by Radio Monte Carlo. The promontory itself (with the

lighthouse and the aerials) cannot be reached; but the wild beauty of its majestic boulders will leave you breathless. From the locked gate you can reach the access road and finally the Agia Napa-Protaras road, to return by taxi or by bus.

Should you wish to carry on to Paralimni (4 additional miles), turn right on the Agia Napa-Protaras road, and after a few hundred yards turn right again toward the **Agia Anargyri Church**. Follow the winding path for less than half a mile, turn left and carry on along the rocky shore to Protaras. After taking in the view at Cape Greco, continue past an ancient cave and an old windmill, until finally reaching Protaras itself, one of Cyprus' gems.

Return to Agia Napa by taxi or by bus.

Beaches

The Agia Napa district has the best beaches on the island. The **Ayia Thekla Beach** is situated 4 miles west of the village; it is a small, relatively isolated beach. The **Makronisos Beach** is much closer to the village – less than one mile away, with three small and pleasant sand coves. The **Nissi Beach**, 2 miles west of the village, is sheltered by the Nissi islot, with a hotel and restaurant cluster, with a wide range of seaside services. The **Sandy Beach** is also very well sheltered and equipped.

The main, and most crowded, Agia Napa Beach is **Golden Sands**, east of the fishermen's pier. It also offers, of course, all the tourist services.

A walk along the beaches, on a beautiful day, is very pleasant indeed. Start from the village towards Sandy Beach; visit the **Agios Georgios Church**, then turn westward to the beaches, where you can enjoy the scenery and the bikinis.

The Golden Sands Beach – many come to soak up the sun

Protaras, less than 6 miles from Agia Napa, also has two excellent beaches: **Flamingo Bay** and **Fig Tree Bay**.

FROM LARNACA TO LIMASSOL

The forty-odd miles that separate Larnaca from Limassol are not very interesting. The crowded, narrow asphalt motorway (a slow and rather enervating drive) goes on for about 20 miles until it joins the Nicosia-Limassol highway.

The **Stavrovouni Monastery** stands on top of a 2,000 feet mount, towering above its rather flat reaches. It is the most ancient and the most sacred monastery in Cyprus, built by St. Helena (mother of Emperor Constantine) in the year 330. Among the most treasured relics preserved in the Monastery is a fragment of "The True Cross", brought over from the Holy Land by the founding Saint. Today the monastery is home to about a dozen monks.

The monastery is less than 30 miles from Larnaca. To get there from Larnaca, leave town westward on the Limassol highway, and after 3 miles, turn right at the road junction, in the direction of Kalon Chorion. Proceed to Agia Anna and the old Nicosia-Limassol road. Here turn left, and the lane will take you to the monastery, which is open to visitors on Sundays only. On weekdays many worshippers come to the

Stavrovouni Monastery, the most ancient monastery in Cyprus

Agia Varvara Monastery

hut installed in front of the monastery gates, to accept the blessing of the local priest.

The monastery is open 8am-noon, 2-5pm (Sept.-March), and 8am-noon, 3-6pm (April-Aug.).

Note: Only men are allowed in the monastery building, and they have to be properly dressed. The use of cameras is prohibited.

If the weather is good and you feel like a pleasant two-hour walk, leave your car at the sign for Spithoudia, on the access road to the monastery. Turn left and follow the path beyond the water-pump. The path climbs the hillside to the top – and to the monastery.

Not far from the Spithoudia sign is a second, smaller monastery – **Agia Varvara**.

LEFKARA

15 miles out of Larnaca on the same road, you will come to Kofinou. Take the turn-off to the right past this village, toward Lefkara.

The road winds through the hills for about 6 miles toward **Pano Lefkara** and **Kato Lefkara** (Upper and Lower Lefkara), two exquisite mountain hamlets. The tourist centre is in Pano Lefkara.

Lefkara is famous for its lace – the *Lefkaritika* lace. You will find it on sale at scores of shops, together with the usual silver and copper objects and other tourist wares. The lace is very expensive indeed, but the delicate and exquisite craftsmanship is certainly worth the expense.

According to a legend, Leonardo da Vinci visited the village in 1481, and purchased a lace cloth for the main altar of the Milan

Duomo. The *Lefkaritika* style was probably imported here in ancient times from Assyria. Much later, the Venetians brought it home, and set up their own lace industry on the island of Burano. In 1889 a local lace school was opened, and Lefkara lace regained much of its ancient renown.

The Lefkarian women can be seen sitting in front of their homes, stitching away at great speed. The women's job is to stitch and their husbands' is to sell.

In Lefkara there is also a Lace and Silver Filigree Museum, open Monday-Saturday, 10am-4pm. Entrance fee. Tel. 04-342326.

Lefkara, a lovely spot between Larnaca and Limassol

CHOIROKOITIA

3 miles past Lefkara, on the Larnaca-Limassol road, a road branches off north-westward to Choirokoitia and the **Choirokoitia Archaeological Site**.

This is the site of the largest Neolithic (5800-3000 BC) settlement in Cyprus, sprawled out on a hillside along the Maroni

River. Its people lived in stone and baked mud huts; they buried their dead under the hut floor. They farmed the land, spun and wove cloth, herded sheep and made earthen tools and effigies. Excavations uncovered signs of raw material apparently imported from Asia Minor. The archaeological findings – amphora fragments, medallions, stone arrowheads and tools etc. – point to a very high level of culture. The site is open to visitors Mon.-Fri. 7.30am-5pm, Sat.-Sun. 9am-5pm. Entrance fee.

AMATHOUS

Five miles before Limassol, on the right hand side of the road, are the fascinating ruins of Amathous. Just before them is a large, modern hotel.

Ornamentation at the Lefkara Church

Amathous was once an opulent town, as witnessed by the ruins of its acropolis, its necropolis (cemetery), a basilica, and ancient harbour.

According to Greek myth, Amathous was founded in the 10th century BC, by Amathous, Heracles' son, and Amathusa, mother of the local king. In one of their raids, the early Moslems sacked the town in the 7th century AD; in the 12th century, an earthquake completely destroyed it and it was never rebuilt. The excavations uncovered objects dating from the 10th century BC to the late Byzantine Era: bronze, silver and gold ornaments, coins and amphoras. A gigantic six foot tall amphora was taken to the Louvres Museum in Paris. According to local lore, the amphora was illegally sold to France in 1862 by the Turkish Sultan. More recent digs uncovered, among other objects, the upper torso of a statue of the Egyptian god Bes, on exhibit at the Limassol Museum.

The ruins of Amathous, once a thriving town

LIMASSOL (LEMESOS)

Limassol has a population of about 135,000 and is the second largest town in Cyprus. Limassol is also Cyprus' main industrial and maritime centre. Here Richard the Lionheart wedded Berengaria of Navarre and crowned her Queen of England. Over the centuries the town was repeatedly invaded and conquered from the sea.

Although Limassol is a busy industrial centre today, many tourists only pass through on their way to more attractive sites. This is perhaps the reason why it has been able to maintain the traditions of Cypriot life. Nevertheless, quaint old boutiques and dark inns are rapidly changing into modern shopping centres and restaurants.

The Limassol promenade

How to Get There

By Sea: Limassol is the main seaport of the island. As we have already mentioned ("How to reach Cyprus"), several shipping lines reach Limassol from Italy, Greece and Israel. The new harbour is in the southern section of the town. No.1 buses and the ubiquitous taxi services connect the harbour with the town centre.

By Land: Buses reach Limassol from all over the island, and stop at one of three main bus stations. The *K.E.M.E.K* buses have their terminal at the Enoseos and Eirinis Sts., north of the castle and not far from the centre and the sea. They include the Nicosia-Limassol line, the Pafos-Limassol and the Polis-Pafos-Limassol lines. For timetable and other information, call Tel. 363241.

The *Kallenos* lines (Tel. 351031) have their terminal at the corner of Araouzou and Hadjipavlou Sts. and they travel to Larnaca and to Agia Napa. The third bus station is used by most urban lines, and is on Andreas Themistokleu St., in the centre of town.

Limassol is also connected to the major island towns by a network of shared-taxi lines. They are faster and more frequent but twice as expensive as the buses. The shared-taxis have their terminals at 49 Spyrou Araouzou St. (*Kypros Co.*, Tel. 363979), or at 21 Thessalonikis St. (*Karydas* and *Kyriakos Co's.*, Tel. 362061).

Tourist Services

The CTO office is at 15 Araouzou St., Tel. 362756. Opening hours: September-May, Monday-Saturday 8.15am-1.45pm; Monday and Thursday also 3-5.30pm. June-August, Monday-Saturday 8.15am-1.30pm, Monday and Thursday also 4-6.15pm.

A CTO Branch Office operates at 35A Odos Georgiou (opposite the west entrance of Dassoudi Beach), Tel. 323211, and at Limassol Port, Tel.

At the new port of Limassol

343868 (the CTO branch in the port opens on arrival of passenger ships).

At the CTO offices you will be able to obtain a Limassol map and various written information. The office staff will also assist you with hotel reservations and travel information.

Urban Transportation

The Central bus station is very central indeed, and the urban network connects it with Limassol's periphery and suburbs. There are also several private taxi stands near the station. Limassol is very crowded, its streets are narrow, parking is scarce and traffic is very slow.

CAR HIRE

At Limassol you will find branches of all the main car hire agencies. *A. Petsas*, *Hertz* and *Avis* are on the Nicosia road; *Europcar* is closer to the city centre.

Hertz: Nicosia Road, G3 Anna Court, Tel. 323758.

Budget: Old Limassol-
Nicosia Road, Sea

Breeze Building, Tel.
323672.

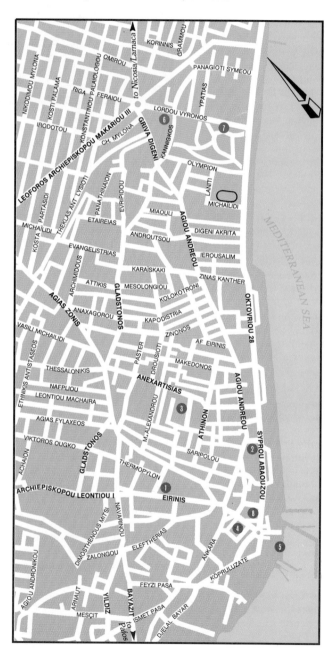

A. *Petsas*: Nicosia Road, Tel. 323672.

Another local car-hire agency, smaller than the island-wide A. *Petsas*, is the *Andy Spyrou* company, with branches also at Pafos and Nicosia. Its offices are on 38-40 Omonia Ave., Tel. 371441. If you have reserved your car in advance, a company driver will meet you, keys in hand, at the gate of the Limassol harbour.

MOTORCYCLE HIRE
Zenmar Trading Ltd.: 144A Makarios III Ave., Tel. 383550.

Nicolaides Nicos: 30 Navarino St., Tel. 369021.

Bicycles can be hired at *Andreas Aristidou*, 1 Leontion Machera, Tel. 364145.

All major Cyprus banks have branches in Limassol. The *Bank of Cyprus* has several branches, most of them downtown, between Spyrou Araouzou St. and Gladstonos and Navarinu. The main branch is at 1 Saripolos St., Tel. 369322. Money changing and other tourist services are also provided in the afternoon at the harbour and at the Agiou Andreou St. branches.

The main post office is on Archiepiskopou Kyprianos St., and the T&T office (open Monday-Saturday, 7am-midnight) is not too far, on Markou Botsarsi St.

Accommodation

As everywhere else in Cyprus, Limassol's cheapest hotels are also the most central ones. Luxury hotels are found along the eastern beaches, and on the Larnaca and Nicosia roads, together with several modern apartment hotels.

5-STAR HOTELS
Amathus Beach: near the Amathous archaeological site, 5 miles from town, Tel. 321152. Relatively expensive, but very well equipped; private beach.

Limassol Sheraton: at

LIMASSOL (LEMESOS)

1. K.E.M.E.K. Terminal
2. Lefkaritis Terminal
3. Central Bus Station
4. Limassol Castle
5. Old Harbour
6. Limassol Archaeological Museum
7. The Zoo
8. CTO Office

Amathous, 7 miles from town, Tel. 321100. Outstanding services, also including a private beach; pricey.

Poseidonia Beach: Old Limassol-Nicosia Rd., Tel. 321000. East of town, towards Nicosia. Very good service, and the prices are somewhat lower.

4-STAR HOTELS

Azur: A Class. Old Limassol-Nicosia Rd., Tel. 322667. East of the town centre; studio apts. and 1 room suites; swimming pool; relatively expensive.

Churchill: 28 Oktovriou St., Tel. 324444. Closer to 5-star hotels both in prices and services. In the eastern suburbs. Private beach, pool and sauna.

Curium Palace: Vyronos St., Tel. 363121. Central – and cheaper. Swimming pool, but no private beach.

Elias Beach: Amathous, 6 miles east of town, Tel. 325000.

Limonia Bay: near the *Amathus Beach* hotel, Tel. 321023. Very attractive prices.

3-STAR HOTELS

Ariadne: 333, 28 Oktovriou St., Tel. 359666. Within the eastern town limits. More expensive than the *Adonia Beach*. Swimming pool, but no beach.

Alasia: 1 Haydari St., near Makarios Ave., at strolling distance from the town centre, Tel. 332000, fax 335424. Swimming pool.

2-STAR HOTELS

Pefkos: a stone's throw from the town centre, 86 Mishaoulis

The old harbour of Limassol

Kavazoglou St., Tel. 377077.
Swimming pool; room air-conditioning an extra.

Chez Nous Sunhotel: on
Potamos Yermassogias St., Tel.
323033. East of the town
centre. Swimming pool and
standard services.

INEXPENSIVE HOTELS

Le Village: 220 A. Leontiou
St., Tel. 368126. 500 yards
west of the town centre.

Panorama: 36 Pavlos Melas
St., Tel. 364667. Central;
closes for the winter and re-
opens in May.

Downtown, between Zinonos
and Anexartisias Sts. there are
some small (10-20 rooms) very
inexpensive hotels; (Some are
open only for the summer
season).

Acropole: 21 Yeorgiou
Malekidi St., Tel. 362706.

Astoria: 13A Yeorgiou
Malekidi St., Tel. 362708.

YOUTH HOSTELS

The only hostel is on 120
Ankara St. (Tel. 363749), just
behind the castle. Open all
year, office hours 7.30am-
11pm.

APARTMENT HOTELS

Renanda: A Class. Amathous,
Tel. 321133. 1-2 room suites.
Air-conditioning and room TV
are extras. Swimming pool.

Atlantica: B Class. Potamos
Germasogia, Tel. 321141.
Rather far from the town
centre; 1-2 room suites;
swimming pool.

Twiga: B Class. 114 Makarios
Ave., Tel. 337236. Very
central, and relatively inexpensive.

CAMPING

Kalymnos Beach Camping
Site: 20km east of Limassol,
with 111 caravans and 250
tents. Tel. 632300.

Restaurants

Limassol has lots of *meze*
restaurants, specially in the
centre and in the eastern
quarter.

Lefieris Tavern is an outstanding *meze* restaurant, in the
village of Germasogia, 4 Agias
Christinis St., Tel. 325211.
Authentic atmosphere, excellent mutton roast; reasonably
priced.

Kanaris is a pleasant and tradi-
tionally styled restaurant

offering meze and international cuisine, 27 Ayias Paraskevis, village of Yermasoyia, Tel. 327303.

Santa Barbara Beach is a fish restaurant on the road to Amathous, Tel. 321046; also bar, snack bar and café; relatively expensive, but its *grilled Haloumi* is outstanding, as are its excellent wines.

Jack's Pizza Place: pizzas and spaghetti, has two branches: 15 Heraclis Michaelides St. and 144 Griva Digeni St., Tel. 342047.

Canadiana Pizza & Spaghetti is at 235H Makarios Ave., Tel. 375555.

Round About Fish & Chips is an English style restaurant and take away on Gr. Digenis St., Limassol Centre. Tel. 358424.

Scotti Steak House, 38 Souli St., corner of Makarios III Ave. (Tel. 335173) is the place to go for an excellent steak.

Chrigiaua on Dionysiou Kykkoti St. and Nicosia Ave., Tel. 324619, is a good sea food restaurant.

WINE AND BEER CELLARS
Limassol is Cyprus' main wine-producing centre. All the island's major cellars are here, and some are open to visitors. Enquire at the CTO for their timetables and addresses.

Shopping
The main shopping areas in Limassol are on Anexartiatis and Agiou Andreou Sts. and Makarios III Ave., which encircles the whole centre of town, from coast to coast: Plenty of footwear and clothing, some electrical appliances and electronics.

There are also some first class jewellry shops; the most prestigious is *Leo Jewelry*, 4 Anexartiasis St., Tel. 355277. Another is *Shakti*, 73, Georgiou A' St., Zoeland Court, Tel. 327624, which sells unique and exclusive hand made accessories.

Night life
Limassol prides itself on being a modern town. It vaunts many new hotels,

apartment hotels, high-rises and restaurants. On Georgiou A. Potamos Yermasogias St., east of the promenade, are the *Caribbean Night Spot & Disco* (Tel. 321868) and the *Triangle Disc* (Tel. 323322).

Near the *Apollonia* hotel, north of the main road on 1 Ampelakia St., is the *Mylos Disco,* Tel. 321777. At 50A Omonia St. you will find the pleasant *Ataliotis Costakis* pub, Tel. 372800.

There are 8 cinemas in Limassol. The *Hollywood Cinema* on 104 Gladstone St., Tel. 362436, has a giant jackpot bingo.

Sports

There are tennis courts at several hotels, and also at the *Sporting Club* (11 Olympion St., Tsiflikoudia, Tel. 359818).

As for diving: *Seamasters:* 54A Franklin Roosevelt, Tel. 359089; the Dassoudi Beach has a water sports centre.

Festivals

Six weeks before Easter, Limassol hosts a ten-day carnival, with numerous entertainers and various amateur groups.

In September Limassol celebrates Dionysos' Wine Festival, jointly sponsored by the major wine and beer cellars.

Useful Phone Numbers

Limassol's area code: 05.
First Aid, Police and Fire Brigade: 199.
Hospital: corner of Leontiou and Gladstonos Sts., Tel. 330156.
Night Pharmacy: Tel. 192.
K.E.M.E.K Bus Lines: corner of Enoseos and Erinis Sts., Tel. 363241.
Kypros taxis: 49 Spyrou Araouzou St., Tel. 363979.
Self service laundromat: 20 Odos Georgiou, Tel. 368293.
Car breakdown emergency service: 4 Leoforos Omonias, Tel. 3553366.
CTO: 15 Spyrou Araouzou St, Tel. 362756; Dassoudi beach, Tel. 323211; Limassol Port, Tel. 343868.
Cyprus Popular Bank: 113 Makarios III Ave., Tel. 335333.

The Limassol promenade at sunset

Sites to See

The main historic site in Limassol is **Limassol Castle**, near the old harbour, Tel. 330419. It is a 12th century structure, restored at a later date by the Venetians. This is where Richard the Lionheart celebrated his wedding to Berengaria of Navarre.

The castle will not sweep you off your feet; in spite of its historical importance, the structure today is not very impressive. It does however contain a very interesting medieval museum. Open Mon.-Fri. 7.30am-5pm and Sat. 9am-5pm. Entrance fee. Tel. 330419.

From the castle, turn to the **old harbour**. In the square, at the corner of Safi and Spyrou Araouzou Sts., you will find a Thai restaurant, a good seafood spot, the *Old Harbour Fish Tavern – Ladas*, and the **Reptile House**. Open 9am-7pm, Tel. 372779, entrance fee.

From the old harbour proceed northwestward, along Spyrou Araouzou St. After a few hundred yards, turn left into one of the alleys and cross to the parallel Agiou Andreou St., where, at No. 2, there is an

Exhibits at the medieval museum located in the Limassol Castle

attractive shopping centre, with a pleasant café under the arches.

Continue northward along Agiou Andreou St. to No. 253, the Folk Art Museum. The museum houses a large selection of authentic Cypriot craftsmanship. Tel. 362303.

Oktovriou St. runs along the shore toward the eastern quarters. About a mile from the old harbour it reaches the city park, which has a small zoo and an open air theatre. The **Limassol Archaeological Museum**, on Lordou Vyronos St., has on exhibit a number of stone axes, knives and arrow heads, tools and various fragments recovered from Amathous and other sites. Also on display are coins and jewels of different periods. The museum is open to the public Mon.-Fri. 7.30am-5pm and 10am-1pm on Sunday. Entrance fee. Tel. 330132.

At Limassol's old harbour

Beaches

Limassol's Dassoudi tourist beach is equipped with adequate services, rest rooms and cafés. If you plan to visit other resorts, don't bother to stop here.

The Limassol District

AKROTIRI

On a sunny day the Akrotiri Peninsula is a very pleasant place for an outing by car or bicycle. Leave town in the direction of Asomatos, passing through the Fassouri vineyards. At Fassouri, turn left to the **Salt Lake**, where flamingoes and other birds of passage come to winter. Twelve miles past the Salt Lake, you will come to the attractive **Lady's Mile** beach.

THE GERMASOGIA DAM

Another pleasant ride is to the Germasogia Dam. Leave Limassol on the Old Nicosia Road (not the highway). After 2.5 miles turn left to the large village of Germasogia. If you have a fishing permit (Tel. 362470), you will be allowed to fish at the dam.

THE TROODOS MOUNTAINS

The road leaves Limassol northward, climbing gradually through the southern reaches of Troodos. A ride of about 30 miles will first take you to **Alassa** and **Platres**, and then to Troodos. There are plenty of attractive picnic areas and scenic stops on the way.

You can reach Troodos by a longer, more scenic, route: leave Limassol on the Pafos road to Erimi, a small village at Episkopi's gates. Visit the impressive **Kolossi Castle** (see "From Limassol to Pafos"). At **Erimi**, turn northward, through Kantou and Agios Amvrosios.

Villagers in traditional clothing

After 12 miles the road changes into a track; 3 miles of bumps and jolts and you will find yourself in **Omodos**, surrounded by what was once Sir John de Brie's Vineyard. The local Wine Festival is held here in August, and on September 14 there is a very colourful religious procession to the Stavros Monastery, which houses icons and wooden effigies. About three miles beyond

Omodos you will come to **Kato Platres**, and, after a left turn, to **Foini**. Here the local villagers make interesting, old-fashioned earthenware by hand, which they are more than willing to sell. The local stream teems with excellent trout; the local mountain wine is more than palatable. Return to Kato Platres, then to **Pano Platres**, and from there again to Limassol.

You may also enjoy a short visit to **Agros**, an attractive summer resort north of Limassol, on the **Phyla**, **Palodeia** and **Kalon Chorion** road.

Greenery at Troodos

FROM LIMASSOL TO PAFOS

The scenic Limassol-Pafos Rd. is a must for those travelling towards Pafos. Wide and well kept, it runs along the seashore, and passes through several beautiful observation-points and historic sites. The first, less than 10 miles off Limassol, is **Kolossi**, the village that gave its name to the most famous castle on the island.

The way from Limassol to Pafos offers some delightful views

KOLOSSI CASTLE

This imposing structure was built in 1191. Exactly one hundred years later the castle became the property of the Order of Saint John of Jerusalem, in whose care it remained for 250 years. It stands in the middle of what is probably the most fertile district on the whole island, to which we owe the splendid *Commandaria* wine. In 1570 the Turks conquered the castle – but did not stop growing and producing its wines for centuries. The district was also the main grower of sugar cane, and exported large quantities of it to Europe. The ancient sugar-mill can still be seen, at the foot of the castle walls.

The castle itself was fully restored in 1933. It has three levels, serviced by a steep winding staircase. In the lobby you will see a picture of the Crucifixion. On the first floor are the kitchens and on the upper floor one can find the commander's hall. The castle can be visited from 1st June to 30th September, daily, between 7.30am-7.30pm; from 1st Oct. to 31st May until 5pm. Entrance fee.

Five miles beyond the Kolossi Castle turn-off is **Episkopi** and the local archaeological site of **Pamboula** (14th-11th century BC ruins and several Bronze Age tombs).

At the Kolossi Castle, built in 1191

Between Episkopi and the beach is the modest Byzantine Chapel of **Agios Hermogenis**. It is an ancient stone cemetery, not very well kept (11th century BC to the Roman period). In one of the tombs a gold sceptre was once found, now exhibited at the Cyprus National Museum of Nicosia.

CURIUM (KOURION)

Five miles past Episkopi the road climbs to **Curium**, a settlement founded more than three thousand years ago by Mycenean immigrants. According to Herodotos, the settlement was founded by Kourieus, son of King Kineras. During the wars between the Greek settlers and the Persians, the town's Greek chieftain Stasanor surrendered the town to the Persians without a struggle. Later, under Alexander the Great, Curium became one of the emperor's major strongholds. In the 4th century AD, the town was repeatedly damaged by earthquakes, and in the 7th century AD it was completely razed by the Arabs.

A mosaic at the archaeological site of Curium

Though the site was discovered toward the end of the 19th century,

The remaining columns of the Roman gladiators' house

the first serious excavations began only in 1933. One of the most important structures uncovered is undoubtedly the theatre, with its fantastic view of the beach and the surrounding hills. It dates from the 2nd century BC. It was restored and reinforced three centuries later, only to be destroyed by a 5th century earthquake. The theatre was fully restored in 1961, and now has two thousand seats and one of Cyprus' best views of the Mediterranean. During the summer, a programme of Greek tragedies and other plays is offered. Also noteworthy are the mosaic floors and the Roman baths.

The **Mosaic of Achilles** is the most interesting of the floors. A visit would not be complete without a stop at the **Roman gladiators' house**, or a good look at the **aqueduct** and at the ruins of the early Christian **basilica**. And at every corner you will see scores of Corinthian capitals and columns.

The site is open 1st June-30th Sept. daily, 7.30am-1.30pm. 1st Oct.-31st May, 7.30am-5pm. Entrance fee.

Two miles beyond Curium on the Pafos road, you will come to the **Ylatis Sanctuary of Apollo**, which for more than ten centuries (from the 8th BC to the 4th AD) was a very influential local centre of power. Near the ruins of the sanctuary you will also recognize the structure of a 2nd century stadium and one of the very earliest Christian basilicas. The sanctuary of Apollo is open to visitors 1st June-30th Sept., daily, 7.30am-7.30pm, and until 5pm between Oct. and May.

The ruins of the Ylatis Sanctuary of Apollo

On the northern side of the Pafos Road you will see the village of **Sotira**, on the slopes of a hill. It was built around the ruins of a

very ancient (third millennium BC) settlement, which has not undergone much research.

To Pafos

After Curium the road leaves the coastline and cuts into the interior. Back to the coast after 12 miles, you will arrive at **Petra tou Romiou**, a majestic boulder high above the sea, the mythical birthplace of the goddess Aphrodite.

Six miles further on (and only 6 miles from Pafos itself) is **Palaia Pafos** (Old Pafos), near the village of Kouklia. According to legend, Old Pafos was founded by Kinares, and destroyed by an earthquake in the 12th century BC. Later, when King Agafanor was returning from the Trojan War, his ships were swept ashore by a storm, and Pafos was rebuilt by the survivors. According to some estimates, over 20,000 lived here, working the copper mines and trading with Greek sailors. In the 4th century BC the last King of Pafos, Nikokles, founded New Pafos. The old city was gradually abandoned and survived only as Aphrodite's sacred grounds. The Goddess' annual festival was, until the advent of Christendom, one of the major events of the region, and indeed of all Greece, with tens of thousands of pilgrims dancing and making merry for several days.

The impressive Petra tou Romiou boulder

The excavation of the **Sanctuary of Aphrodites** began in 1888 and continued sporadically for more than a century. The various strata cover a period from the 9th century BC to the 5th century AD.

In addition to the sanctuary, the dig also uncovered a wall and the foundations of a large building, perhaps a hostel for pilgrims. The Sanctuary is open 7.30am-7.30pm between June-Sept., and 7.30am-5pm between Oct.-May. Tel. 432180. Entrance fee.

Near the Police Post of **Kouklia** you will see the ruins of a Roman structure. Its unique mosaic floor is now exhibited at the **Kouklia Museum** together with several amphoras and other findings. More precious findings, including ancient gold coins and jewels, can be viewed at the **Nicosia Archaeological Museum**. A 1987 digs uncovered many additional gold ornaments and objects, and a rare bronze basin decorated with an 11th century BC Greek inscription.

On arrival in Pafos you will pass through the village of **Geroskipou**, famous for its "Turkish Delight" candy, and a small art museum (see "Around Pafos").

Vineyards on the way from Limassol to Pafos

PAFOS

Pafos is the capital of Cyprus' western region. It has a population of about 28,000, most of whom are employed in various branches of tourism. Pafos is very popular with tourists, and specially with German and Scandinavian tourists. Among its attractions are its old harbour, its ancient mosaic floors, and its modern restaurants and hotels, set out along the seaside promenade. And the main shopping lane, which runs parallel to the promenade, is the ideal tourists' marketplace.

The Pafos promenade at sunset

Nea Pafos (New Pafos) was founded in the 4th century BC, 10 miles west of Old Pafos. The new city began to grow only centuries later until it practically replaced its old namesake, and, with the decline of Salamis, became the capital of western Cyprus. When St. Paul brought the message of Christ to Pafos in the year 45, he was lashed and imprisoned. In the end, however, he converted the Roman governor himself, along with most of the population.

Pafos was destroyed twice, by a 1st century earthquake, and in the 7th century, by Arab raiders.

In the 13th century, under the de Lusignans, Pafos became a bishopric seat, but this did not prevent its people from leaving their town to seek more attractive dwellings in the neighbouring hills. Thus Ktima gradually replaced Pafos as the main regional centre. Today Ktima has been practically incorporated into Pafos itself. This is where the city administration is located, as are all major office buildings.

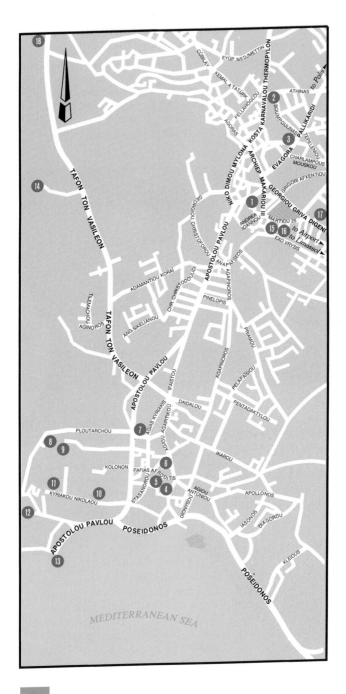

The Leoforos Apostolou Pavlou (St. Paul) Ave. connects Ktima with New Pafos (also known as Kato Pafos, or Lower Pafos), where the town's best hotels and residences, tourist beaches and archaeological sites are located.

How to Get There

By Air: Although Pafos is only a small town, it has its own airport, serving hundreds of thousands of European tourists who come in by charter flights from Western and Northern Europe. The airport is less than 10 miles from town. For information, Tel. 236833.

By Sea: Regular shipping lines do not dock at Pafos harbour, but hundreds of private yachts frequent the local marina.

By Land: The *K.E.M.E.K* bus lines (Tel. 234255) connect Pafos with all the island's main centres: Limassol, Larnaca (via Limassol) and Nicosia (via Limassol). Buses leave Limassol for Pafos approximately every three hours.

The *K.E.M.E.K* terminal is in Ktima, on Fellahoglou St. At the corner of Athinas and

Thermopylon Sts. is the bus stop for Lower Pafos.

The Pafos-Polis line belongs to the *Fontana Amoroza Bus Company*; its buses leave every hour on the hour (but you are advised to make reservations, Tel. 236740).

Special buses connect Pafos with Coral Bay and with Pyrgos (*ALEPA* bus company, Tel. 234252).

Shared-taxi lines (*Karydas* and *Kypros* taxi companies.) run from Pafos to Polis and Limassol and vice versa.

PAFOS
1. *CTO Office*
2. *K.E.M.E.K. Terminal*
3. *Fontana Amoroza Terminal*
4. *St. Paul's Pillar*
5. *Chrysopolitissa Church*
6. *Frankish Bath*
7. *Agia Solomoni Catacombs*
8. *The Lighthouse*
9. *Roman Audion*
10. *Saranta Kolones*
11. *House of Dionysus*
12. *Villa of Theseus*
13. *Old Port & Castle*
14. *Tombs of the Kings*
15. *Ethnographic Museum*
16. *Byzantine Museum*

Tourist Services

The **CTO** Office is located at 3 Odos Gladstonos St., Tel. 232841. The airport branch, Tel. 422833, opens according to incoming times. At the CTO you will find lots of pertinent information, as well as hotel reservation services.

Along the promenade (Poseidonos Ave.), you will find the branches of different banks. The *Bank of Cyprus*, (main office: 13 Evagoras St., Tel. 233078), generally opens for money changing also in the afternoon. The airport bank branch is open around-the-clock. Tel. 233078.

The Lower Pafos Post Office is on Agiou Antoniou St., slightly north of the *Dyonisos* Hotel and the above mentioned branch of the *Bank of Cyprus*. The Main Post Office is in Upper Pafos, on Leoforos Evagora Pallikaridi St., Tel. 240223.

Urban Transportation

The city bus station, which connects the various sections of town, is located in Ktima, on the corner of Athinas and Thermopylon Sts.

CAR HIRE
Here are the addresses of local car hire branches:

Europcar: 77 Poseidonos St., Tel. 234149.

Hertz: 54A Apostolou Pavlou Ave., Tel. 233985.

A. Petsas: Apostolou Pavlou Ave., Tel. 235522.

MOTORCYCLE HIRE
S.P. Christoforou: Poseidonos St., across from the *Sodap* Cellars, Tel. 242672.

Accommodation

All Pafos hotels and apartment hotels are located in Lower Pafos, and are very close to one another. The best hotels are along the beach.

During the summer season (June through October) advance reservation is a must.

5-STAR HOTELS
Imperial Beach: on the Poseidonos promenade, Tel. 245415. Indoor swimming pool, golfing and winter sports facilities.

A hotel in Pafos

4-STAR HOTELS
Annabelle: also on the promenade, Tel. 238333. Excellent services; private beach; relatively high-priced.

Cypria Maris: at the far end of the promenade, Tel. 238111. Somewhat cheaper; all-year (heated) swimming pool – and private beach.

Amalthia Beach Hotel: on the beach, north of the airport. Bungalows and luxurious suites, swimming pool and private beach. Tel. 247777, fax 245963.

3-STAR HOTELS
Aloe: promenade, Tel. 234000. Not really close to the sea; large swimming pool, quiet and relaxing atmosphere; cottage style building; reasonably priced.

Dionysos: 1 Dionysos St., Tel. 233414. Central. No private beach; swimming pool and scenic view of the sea.

Cynthiana Beach: located 5 miles north of Pafos, on Coral Bay Road, Tel. 233922. Private beach and swimming pool.

2-STAR HOTELS
Apollo: Leoforos Apostolou Pavlou, between Ktima and Lower Pafos, Tel. 233909. 500 yards from the beach; swimming pool.

Theofano: Danaes St., on the road to the airport in eastern Lower Pafos, half a mile from the centre of town. Swimming pool. Tel. 233570.

INEXPENSIVE HOTELS AND PENSIONS
Kinyras: Ktima, 89 Leoforos Makariou III, Tel. 233210.

Pelican Inn: 102 Apostolou Pavlou Ave., Tel. 234303.

YOUTH HOSTELS
Ktima, 37 Elftheriou Venizelou, Tel. 232588, open all year; office hours 7.30-10am and 4-11pm.

APARTMENT HOTELS

Daphne: 3 Alkiminis, Tel. 233500. A Class. Studio apts. and 1-2 room suites. Swimming pool, but no private beach, although situated by the sea.

Demetra: Artemidos St., Tel. 234444. Central, studio apts and 1-2 room suites. A Class.

Mirofori: Constantias St., Tel. 234311. Central, near the Post Office; not near the beach. Studio apts., 1 room suites; swimming pool. B Class.

Theseas: 1-3 Jasonos St., Tel. 235511. Central, and near the beach. Slightly higher priced than the *Mirofori*, 1-2 room suites. Swimming pool. B Class.

CAMPING

Geroskipou Zenon Gardens Camping site is located at the Geroskipou tourist beach, 2 miles east of the harbour. Space for 95 tents and trailers; services include showers, toilets, mini market, snack-bar and electrical sockets. Open March to October, Tel. 242277. Feggari Camping Site is situated 16km north-west of Pafos near Coral Bay. Tel. 621534.

Restaurants

The promenade offers a wide choice of *meze* restaurants, all more or less similarly priced. Dining at the old harbour restaurants is pleasant, and you can enjoy lovely views and cool fresh air.

Kyklamino is rather far off, but also far-out; worth the ride: on Pyramos St., Tel. 237766.

Mediterranean Tavern and Restaurant, at 3 Agias Napas St., Tel. 235684, serves both an international and *meze* menu.

Marigold, at 4 Aristi Court, offers take away fish and chips at excellent quality.

At 3-4 Poseidonos Ave. you will find a *pizza parlour and cafeteria* (Tel. 235816).

Shopping

Most shops are located on Makariou III Ave., in Ktima. The shopping facilities in Pafos leave much to be desired. The open market is at the north end of the avenue.

Opening hours are, in winter, 8am-1.30pm and 2.30-5.30pm; in summer 8am-1pm and 4-7pm. On Wednesday and Saturday afternoons most shops remain closed.

The *Cyprus Handicrafts Service* is located at the Agios Theodoros and Gladstonos Sts. corner; it offers a wide selection of local handicrafts.

Pottery can be obtained from the *Lemba Pottery* gallery in the village of Lemba, Tel. 243822. Here one can find, among other things, original vases, lamps, mugs and plates.

Night life

Night life in Pafos belongs to its tourists. Almost every 4-star hotel has its own disco. There are a few cinemas in the city. The most popular pub is the *Pelican Pub* (30 Aphroditis St., Tel. 246886).

However, the major and most popular night life activity in Pafos remains the traditional late evening stroll along the promenade. You can get some refreshments at one of the many cafés that are scattered here.

Sports

Pafos' water sports centres are located along the tourist beach. For diving try:

Annabelle Diving Centre: Pafos Beach, P.O.Box 136, Kato Pafos, Tel. 233091.

Aloe Divers: Aloe hotel, Kato Pafos, Tel. 234000.

Festivals

The main event is the sports and culture festival of *Pampaphia*.

During the month of May, the whole village seems to bloom

with the flower festival which is celebrated by parades and other festivities, along with the 6 calender holidays lining this 3-month period.

Useful Phone Numbers

Pafos area code: 06.
Airport information:
  Tel. 236833.
Ambulance, police and fire
  brigade: Tel. 199.

Hospital: Neofytou Nikolaidi
  St., Upper Pafos. Tel. 240111.
Police Post: Georgiou Griva
  St., Upper Pafos. Tel. 240140.
CTO: 3 Gladstonos St.,
  Tel 232841; airport branch,
  Tel. 236833.
Car breakdown emergency
  service: 22 Odos Manis,
  Tel. 233842.
Self service laundromat: 19
Odos Agiou, Kato Pafos,
  Tel. 246912.
Bank of Cyprus: Dionysou
  Ave., lower Pafos,
  Tel. 233078 – and at the
  airport, Tel. 236962.

Sites to See

Pafos is full of interesting sites, all in the lower, old city.

Lower Pafos

We will start at the intersection of the shopping lane (which runs parallel to the promenade) and Apostolou Pavlou St. Proceed eastward along the promenade to the first left turn (near the *Daphne Hotel*), onto Alkiminis St. Walk up and then make the second left turn. On your right you will see the well preserved early Christian **basilica**. You need a little bit of luck to visit it: it has no regular

Wine tasting in Pafos

opening hours. An imposing Gothic church, destroyed in the 16th century, once stood near the basilica. Here you will see **St. Paul's Pillar**. According to tradition, St. Paul was tied to it and lashed by the Roman governor of Pafos. Further on, in the same street, is the beautiful **Chrysopolitissa Church**. Further on is the

Frankish Bath; only a few fragments remain of the old baths, but their discovery was of considerable archaeological importance. Now return to Apostolou Pavlou Ave., and turn right to St. Paul St. For the **Agia Solomoni Catacombs**, which during the Byzantine Period were also used as a church.

Follow the avenue, and after the *Apollon Hotel* turn right into the narrow Ploutarchou St., which climbs to the **lighthouse**. From here you will enjoy a wonderful panoramic view of Pafos. A reconstruction of a 1st century **Roman Audion** is located near the lighthouse; today it serves as an open air dance and music centre. Turn south along the path, and the next east-west road will take you to **Saranta Kolones**, the ruins of a large Byzantine palace of the 7th century.

At the end of Kyriakou Nikolaou you will see a sort of large loft, where the incomparable floor fragments of the **House of Dionysus** are kept. These 4th century mosaics belonged to the residential palace of the Roman governor; they shed light on various aspects of local daily life and depict the major figures of Greek mythology.

One of the mosaics depicts Dionysus (better known as Bacchus, the god of wine) on his panther-driven chariot and surrounded by a host of satyrs. Another mosaic illustrates the origins of wine: at one end Dionysus himself is happily sipping his godly nectar; at the other end two shepherds lie drunk at the feet of King Ikros, the first mortal whom Dionysus taught the divine art of wine making. Waking up from their drunken stupor, the two peasants, convinced that the king had tried to poison them, murdered the

A mosaic at the House of Dionysus

king on the spot. Other mosaics depict love and hunting scenes, duels and races. One shows a dying horse, falling prey to a panther's claws. Unique among all that violence is the idyllic scene of a vine harvest.

A Hellenistic mosaic of the 4th century BC was discovered, past the grounds of the palace, on its north side. The mosaic shows the two mythical monsters of Charybdis and Scylla of Homeric renown, lying in ambush in the waters of the Messina straits. Scylla's upper torso and face are those of an extremely beautiful woman; but her other half is a scaled monstrosity, part fish and part crab.

The site is open to visitors Mon.-Fri. 7.30am-5pm, Sat.-Sun. 9am-5pm. Entrance fee. Tel. 240217. The local museum is only open on Tuesdays, 7.30am-1.30pm.

Near the House of Dionysus you will see the **Villa of Theseus**, also full of interesting mosaic floors. A round mosaic (which apparently was the floor of a round hall) illustrates Theseus' battle against the Minotaur (Chrete's terrible mythological monster). The floor of the main hall depicts Achilles' birth, with his parents – Thetys and Peleos, witnessing his almost total immersion (with the fateful exception of his heel). Site and local museum follow the timetable of Dionysus' House. Entrance fee.

Visiting wine cellars

From the Villa of Theseus turn southward to the towering **old port and castle**. Today Pafos' old port is completely submerged, probably as a result of one of the frequent earthquakes that plagued the region in ancient times. In 1959 a team of British divers recovered from the shallow sea floor several fragments and objects belonging to the old harbour. Today the site is marked by two large boulders. The small breakwater fort belongs to the de Lusignan Epoch (13th century AD). Destroyed by the Venetians, the fort was rebuilt by the Turks in 1586. It is open to visitors Mon.-Fri. 7.30am-2.30pm, Thurs. 3-6pm, Sat.-Sun. 9am-5pm. Entrance fee.

Along the old port are several restaurants and cafés, which provide perfect backdrop for a welcome break and meal.

Turn eastward to the corner of Apostolou Pavlou, where you started your walk, and stroll eastward along the promenade, stopping to admire the crowds and the attractive shop windows.

The Tombs of the Kings

Approximately 2.5 miles north of the old port are the Tombs of the Kings (Tafon ton Vasileon). If this is too far for you to walk, there is always the bus. Walk northward along Apostolou Pavlou Ave., and follow it to the road sign that points left toward the site. The tombs are impressive enough to be worthy of kings – even if they are not. They are burial caves carved into the bedrock of the hill, and decorated with doric columns and capitals; they date from the 4th century BC. The site is open Mon.-Fri. 7.30am-5pm, Sat.-Sun. 9am-5pm. Entrance fee. Tel. 240295.

Ktima

Today Ktima – or Upper Pafos – is the district capital. In the past, it was the burial grounds for new Pafos – or lower Pafos. "Ktima" in Greek means "property".

There are several small but interesting museums here. The **Ethnographic Museum** is at 1 Exo Vrisi, near the seat of the Pafos archbishopric. It contains a collection of costumes and other objects characteristic of Cypriot daily life over the centuries. Opening hours are 9am-1pm and 2-5pm on Mon.-Sat., between May-Sept. 2-5pm only and Sun. 10am-1pm. Tel. 232010. the afternoon hours are 3-5pm. On Sunday, only 10am-1pm. Entrance fee. The **Archaeological Museum** of Pafos is on Georgiou Griva Digeni. It exhibits ancient Neolithic and Bronze Age idols; amphoras from various periods; statues, statuettes and fragments from local digs and the statues of Dionysus and Esculapios from the House of Dionysus. Open in summer Mon.-Fri. 7.30am-2.30pm and 4-6pm; in winter, Mon.-Fri. 7.30am-2.30pm and 3-5pm. Sunday 10am-1pm all year. Entrance fee. Tel. 240215.

The **Byzantine Museum** is at the archbishopric seat, not far from the Ethnographic Museum, on 25 Martiou St. (south of the city garden). It belongs to the Greek-Orthodox Church. The museum's collection of icons is outstanding. Open June-September, Mon.-Sat., 9am-1pm and 4-7pm ; the rest of the year afternoon hours are 2.30-5.30pm. Entrance fee. Tel. 232092.

Pafos' sunny seaside promenade, a perfect place for rest

Geroskipou

Three miles east of Pafos is the Cyprus home of *Loukoumia* (Turkish Delight) – the picturesque village of Geroskipou.

Its **Agia Paraskevi Church** is one of the best examples of Byzantine architecture in Cyprus. It is a five-domed structure of the 11th century, with each dome forming a separate chapel, with some beautiful and well-preserved 15th century frescoes.

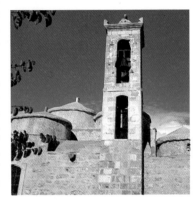

An old residence houses the **Folklore Museum**, and contains a number of old looms, tools and woodwork. Open on weekdays, in summer 7.30am-1.30pm and in winter until 2pm (Saturday only until 1pm). Entrance fee. Tel. 240216.

The Beach

The Pafos tourist beach is situated east of lower Pafos, in the direction of the airport and Geroskipou. The hotels' private beaches line the strip below the promenade.

Around Pafos

NORTHWARD ALONG THE SHORE

The western coast roads are most suitable for bicycle rides. Take the Polis Road through the Tombs of the Kings, and turn left to **Coral Bay** and its beach, which is an excellent skin-diving spot, with a pleasant café. North of the bay is the village of **Pegeia** with some unusual fountains and water jets on its main square.

Now leave the Polis Road and turn left (westward) to **Cape Drepanon**, with the ruins of the Agios Georgios Basilica and several old burial caves near a tiny fisher-

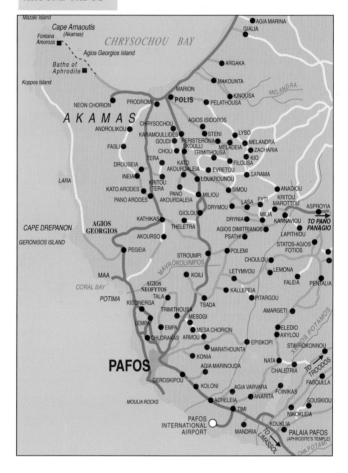

men's village. Three miles beyond the Cape is the **Lara Bay**, with one of Cyprus' best beaches.

Polis

Polis is a small town on the **Chrysochou Bay**, about 25 miles north of Pafos, with a startlingly beautiful fishing harbour. It was built on the site of the ancient Marion, a Hellenistic trade and cultural centre, prosperous thanks to its rich copper and gold mines. The Syrians changed its name to

Arsinoe, a name it kept for several centuries, throughout the Byzantine Period. Today it has become one of Cyprus' summer resorts. It has several small and inexpensive hotels, both in town and along the western beach.

Elia is an A Class apartment hotel overlooking the sea, equipped with a swimming pool and good tennis courts (Tel. 321011). The *Polis Camping* (Tel. 321526) is in an eucalyptus grove by the sea, 500 yards from the town. It has 200 tent or trailer sites, and is fully serviced with showers, toilets, mini market, first aid and electrical sockets. Small tents for hire. Open from March to October, Tel. 321526.

Arsinoe Water Sports is a diving club, Tel. 06-321216.

The site of the **Baths of Aphrodite** is less than six miles east of Polis. This is the mythical site where the goddess of beauty used to bathe in the "fountain of youth". We cannot guarantee the results, but you might give it a try – and enjoy the scenery: a small rocky pool hidden on the mountain-side, framed by fig trees and evergreens.

Near Cape Arnaoutis (a.k.a. Cape Akamas), 3 miles further on north-westward, is

The harbour in Pafos

another legend: that of the **Fontana Amorosa** (The Fountain of Love); all those who drink its waters are supposed to fall instantly in love.

The Fountain of Love cannot be reached by car: you will have to board a boat from Latchi (west of Polis) or walk along the path crossing the rocky coast of the bay from the Baths of Aphrodite to the fountain. However, be warned: this area is used frequently by the Cyprus Army for its training exercises, and a military clearance must be obtained beforehand (for information, call the CTO).

From Pafos to Troodos

There is no regular transportation service between Pafos and Troodos. The following routes are, therefore, only for private and rented cars, or by special taxi.

First itinerary: this is the standard route. It is more direct, quicker but less rewarding. Leave Pafos on the Limassol Road, and follow the Troodos road signs. You may leave the coastal road towards Troodos slightly before coming to Kouklia (old Pafos), in the direction of **Nikokleia** and **Arsos**, or take the turnoff to **Prastion**. The two segments join up before reaching Platres, on the way to Troodos. There is little to see on the way, except for the countryside, covered with vineyards and specked with isolated farms and small hamlets. If you take the Prastion route, after 12 miles you will come to **Omodos**. August is the time of the harvest festival in Omodos, and the village monastery (Stavros Monastery) holds a procession on 14th September.

A turn left will take you from Kato Platres, a few miles beyond Omodos, to **Foini**, a small village famous for its traditional handmade earthenware.

Second itinerary: this route takes you from Pafos to Troodos along winding asphalt lanes and mountain tracks, passing through many interesting sites.

Leave Pafos on the Polis Road, crossing Mesogi and Tsada. Slightly before Stroumpi turn right at the turnoff to **Pano Panagia**. The road is difficult and bumpy; it climbs 3,000 feet to Pano Panagia and offers some of the most impressive sights on the island. Pause at one of the mountain hamlets to observe the Cypriot mountain farmers at their toil.

From Pano Panagia proceed on the eastward track, towards the **Kykkos**

Monastery (see "The Troodos Mountains"). It is a 20 mile drive from Pano Panagia to the Monastery, without a single sign of human habitation. There are several turnoffs, each with its road sign; there are other access roads to the Monastery, but it's better to follow the road signs rather than any eventual suggestions by local "experts".

The road continues eastward to Pedoulas, where it turns southward, near the TV aerials of Mount Troodos (6,150 feet) toward the Troodos.

THE TROODOS MOUNTAINS

The region of the Troodos Mountains, covering most of the central mass of Cyprus, attracts many people; the green slopes, dotted with tiny villages, the forest paths, the cool weather, the ancient monasteries, some dating back to the Byzantine period, and the hospitable, friendly local population make a visit here an extremely pleasant experience. This is the place where one can meet traditional Cyprus. The higher peaks reach 6,000 feet; the highest, Mt. Olympos, is 6,403 feet high.

The "capital" of the district is **Troodos**, a small village, which has little to offer the tourist. The larger centre – **Platres** (6 miles from Troodos) – has quite a wide selection of hotels, restaurants and shopping facilities to offer. Platres climbs to a height of about 3,500 feet, on the southern slopes of Mt. Olympos, and is surrounded by pine forests. Platres is an excellent winter sports centre, with convenient access to the Mt. Olympos ski-runs. Also the southern beaches are not very far – half an hour ride by car or taxi. As the the local saying goes: "What is your choice: mountain-ski or water-ski?"

The winter-ski season generally lasts through January and February, and is centered in Troodos. Summer tourism is also very popular (based mainly in Platres).Average temperatures in February reach about 4°C (40°F); in August temperatures rarely climb above 30°C (85°F).

The Troodos Mountains

How to Get There

A private car is very convenient for reaching Platres, as there are no shared-taxi lines and no local buses. The "carless" traveller will have to manage with inter-urban bus stops, special taxis, and good walking shoes.

From Nicosia: the *K.E.M.E.K* (Tel. in Nicosia: 02-463154) bus leaves the Capital for

THE TROODOS MOUNTAINS

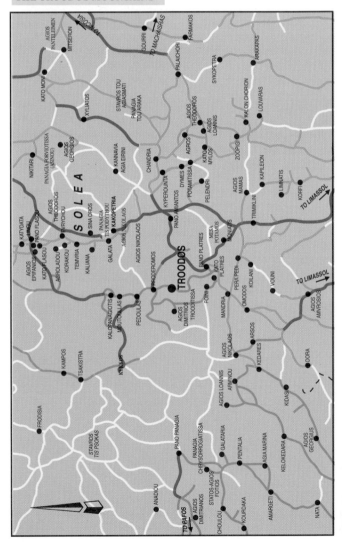

Platres at 12.15am daily. The return trip goes through Kalopanagiotis and Pedoulas. The Troodos *Solea Bus* (Tel. in Nicosia: 02-462825) leaves Nicosia daily at 12am (from the Constanza Bastion stop, 200 yards from Eleftheria Sq.).

The *Solea Bus* company also runs the Nicosia-Kakopetria line (Kakopetria is 8 miles from Troodos). The *K.E.M.E.K* line also makes a daily run from Nicosia to the Kykkos Monastery. For detailed information, call the Nicosia CTO.

From Limassol: The *Karydas* (Tel. in Limassol: 05-362061) bus leaves for Platres at 12.45am. In July and August there may be additional runs; call the company for details. *K.E.M.E.K* also runs a daily bus to Platres; the return trip leaves Platres at 1.00pm for Prodromos, Pedoulas and Limassol. A special bus leaves Limassol at 11.45am for Agros, another mountain resort, east of Troodos.

There are no other regular bus connections with the Troodos mountains.

Tourist Services

The mountain region is not densely populated, and its resorts are less popular than its beaches. Tourist services are also less devel-

The traditional means of transportation in the Troodos Mountains

oped. The closest hospital is in Limassol.

The only **CTO** branch is in Platres (open from the middle of May to the end of September, Main Square, Tel. 421316). Here you will find a map of the region and a pamphlet map-ping out some interesting walks. The post office and a bank (Tel. 421719) are also in the main square. None of the car-hire agencies has a branch in the mountains.

Four other bank branches can be found in the Troodos Mountains region, located at Kakopetria, Pedoulas, Kyper-ounta and Prodromos.

and are very close to one another.

Forest Park: 4 stars. Tel. 421751. The only hotel offering not only heated rooms, but a heated pool, TV, air-conditioning, mini-bar and conference room. Panoramic view.

Edelweiss: Tel. 421335. 2 stars; heated rooms.

Minerva: Tel. 421731. 1 star. Central heating, air-conditioning, TV and telephone. Some of these services cost an extra sum.

Splendid: Tel. 421424. 1 star, central heating.

Kalithea: Tel. 421746. Modest, 28 beds.

Mount Royal: Tel. 421345. Modest, 25 beds.

Accommodation

There are several hotels in Platres, with others located in the neighbouring villages. They are simple establishments, not as well equipped as their seaside counterparts, but they are generally pleasant, well serviced and clean. Following is a list of some of the local hotels:

PLATRES
Platres area code: 05.

All hotels are centrally located

TROODOS
Troodos area code: 05

Jubilee: Tel. 421647. 2 stars, central heating.

Troodos: Tel. 421635. 2 stars, central heating.

The **Youth Hostel** is located 400 yards from the village, on the Troodos-Nicosia Road (Tel. 422400); open July and August. Office hours 7.30-10.30am and 4-12pm.

The **Camping-Site** is at little more than 1 mile from the village, on the Kakopetria

Road. Equipped with showers, toilets, restaurant and bar, mini market and first aid. Open from end-May to October. Tel. 421624. The nights are very cold; come well prepared.

KAKOPETRIA
Kakopetria area code: 02.

Hellas: Tel. 922450. 3 stars, central heating.

Hekali: Tel. 922501. 2 stars, central heating.

Krystal: Tel. 922433. 2 stars, central heating.

Kyfissa: Tel. 922421. Very modest.

PEDOULAS
Pedoulas area code: 02.

The Churchill Pinewood Valley: Tel. 952211; services include central heating, pool, tennis courts and sauna (3 stars).

Marangos: Tel. 952657. No central heating; 2 stars.

Jack's: Tel. 952350, central heating; 1 star.

AGROS
Agros area code: 05.

Rodon: Tel. 521201. 3 stars, central heating and heated pool.

Vlachos: Tel. 521330. 1 star.

Restaurants
Most villages have several *meze* restaurants; in Troodos you will find two modest restaurants, and in Platres you will find more than ten along a 200-yard strip on the main road.

Winter sports
In winter, the Troodos mountain hotels turn into winter sport resorts: the Mt. Olympos slopes and ski-runs are generally open for skiing throughout January and February, and often also in March. The runs are 7 miles from Platres, and can also be reached from Nicosia or Limassol in less than an hour.

A ski cabin in the Troodos Mountains

The Cyprus Ski Federation (P.O.Box 2185, Nicosia, Tel. 02-365340, fax 02-448777), offers permanent and temporary membership subscriptions. The Mt. Olympos ski-runs are serviced by 4 ski lifts: two on the northern side and two along the southern Sun Valley. The northern (350 yard long) runs are for experienced skiers, the Sun Valley runs (150 yard only) are for beginners.

In Sun Valley you will also find a fully equipped winter sports store that offers equipment for sale and hire. There are cafeterias and rest-rooms at the end of all the runs.

PICNIC SITES
Along the hillsides of the Troodos mountains are many picnic grounds, most along the main roads and tracks. If you are motoring, bring your own water and food.

Pedoulas – a typical mountain village in the Troodos

Trips by Car

The Northern Slopes

Leave Pano Platres southward, toward Kato Platres (not on the Limassol main road!). At Kato Platres take the side road to **Foini**, a small attractive village where craftsmen turn out traditional earthenware without the help of modern technology.

From Foini take the northern track; after 2 miles it joins the Pano-Platres – Prodromos Road. Turn left toward Prodromos; after little more than a mile you will see the **Trood-hitissa Monastery**, which is in fact an 18th century church built on the foundations of a 13th century monastery. In the church are several icons and a statuette of the Virgin

Mary, of Asian origins. The site is usually open from 12am-2pm. Do not enter in shorts (or immodest clothing!). Simple accommodation is available; no fixed payment is required, but donations are welcome.

Prodromos is a popular summer resort, on the slopes of the second highest Troodos peak. It is the seat of Cyprus' Forestry College.

The entrance to the Kykkos Monastery

From Prodromos, the road proceeds to **Pedoulas**, which is another summer resort, famous for its cherries. In the **Michael Archangel Church** you will find some interesting 15th century works of art. The church is generally locked; keys are available next door on request. Pedoulas, Moutoullas and Kalopanagiotis are three villages perched on the slopes of the beautiful Marathasa Valley.

A corridor in the Kykkos Monastery

Seven miles east of Pedoulas is the famous **Kykkos Monastery**. This monastery, more than 4,000 feet high, is one of Cyprus' highlights. Built in 1100 and dedicated to the Virgin Mary, it is one of the most ancient and richest monasteries in Cyprus. In the courtyard are mosaics illustrating the Crucifixion, the Nativity, the Resurrection and other miracles. In the main hall are two ancient icons, attributed to St. Lucas. An icon of the Virgin Mary, held in a special alcove, is believed to have miraculous powers. Archbishop Makarios III completed his ecclesiastic studies here; on his death, he was buried at Throni, two miles from the Monastery.

Note: dress properly, or accept the

One of the several churches in Galata

heavy mantles offered at the entrance. You may not photograph inside the monastery.

Moutoullas is less than 1.5 mile north of Pedoulas; its church dates from the 13th century, and it has some very interesting frescoes. Its wooden roof is one of the earliest of its type; the church keys are available next door.

If you feel like visiting one more church, you may visit **Agios Ioannis Lampadistis**, in Kalopanagiotis, less than a mile further north. This church, which was also a former monastery, has some interesting 13th-15th century frescoes. Keys to the church can be obtained either at the monastery, or in the house next to the bridge. The village is also famous for its sulphur springs. The next villages, **Galata** and **Kakopetria**, are further down the mountain slopes, in the Solea district. You will find a turn-off to **Linou** about 7 miles from Kalopanagiotis.

A mosaic in the Kykkos Monastery, dedicated to the Virgin Mary

Past Pano Flasou and Evrychou the side road joins up with the Nicosia-Troodos main road. Turn right, and after a 4 mile ride southward, you will come to Galata and Kakopetria, two pleasant villages, each with a Byzantine church.

In fact, Galata has no less than three churches: the **Panagia Theotokos Church** (or Church of the Angel), a 12th century structure, decorated in the interior with 16th century frescoes; the **Panagia Podithou Church**, built in 1512; and the **Agios Sozomenos Church**, also a 16th century building with post-Byzantine frescoes, the keys for which can be found with the priest (enquire at one of the local cafés).

Agios Nicolaostis Stegis Church

Beyond Galata you will reach Kakopetria, where you may turn off southwestward (for less than two miles) to the **Agios Nicolaostis Stegis**, another church built on the foundations of an earlier monastery. Today the church is somewhat neglected. Open Monday-Saturday 9am-4pm; Sunday only from 9.30am.

Leave Kakopetria by the main Nicosia-Troodos Road to return to Troodos and Pano Platres.

East of Troodos

This itinerary will take you from Pano

Platres to the eastern Troodos Plateau and back.

Leave Pano Platres on the main road, turning left toward Kakopetria; about half-way to the village, turn right following the road signs to **Kyperounta**, 3 miles away. Cross this rather large village and proceed to Chandria, and then further on to **Lagoudera**. Here you will find the 12th century **Panagia tou Araka Church**, one of the most famous churches in Cyprus. Constructed of stone and wood, it is a charming place with splendid frescoes.

Turn back from Lagoudera through Polystipos and **Alona**. Having crossed Alona, turn left to **Platanistasa**. Two miles past this village is the **Stavros tou Agiasmati Church**, with several 15th century frescoes.

Return to the Alona turn-off and proceed eastward through Fterikoudi and Askas to **Palaichori**, a village renowned for its pork sausages (*loukanica*) and its smoked pork (*chiromeri*). The village also offers two more interesting churches: the **Panagia Chrysopantanassa** (16th century) and the **Sotiros Church** (15th century).

The magnificent interior of the Panagia tou Araka Church

The Nicosia Road now turns north-eastward to Apliki, and, slightly off to your right, Gourri and Lazanias, where the **Machairas Monastery** is hidden.

This monastery is situated at almost 3,000 feet above sea level, on the eastern slopes of the Troodos Mountains, in a deep pine tree forest. It was founded in the 12th century as the receptacle of a holy icon of the Virgin Mary, found pierced by a sword (in Greek, sword – machaira), by two local monks.

In 1892 the building was almost completely destroyed by fire, and very little remains of its legendary treasures. After the fire it was rebuilt, and become famous once again in 1957. Gregoris Afxendiou, one of Colonel Grivas' Eoka fighters (see "History"), who had been hiding on the monastery grounds, was discovered by the British; to avoid being taken prisoner he burnt himself to death.

The road from Machairas to Nicosia passes through the archaeological site of Tamassos (see "From Troodos to Nicosia").

If you'd rather go back towards Palaichori and Troodos, you will have the opportunity to visit **Agros**, one of the best mountain resorts. Here a side road will take you northward to **Chandria**, and from there to Kyperounta and Troodos or Pano Platres.

Machairas Monastery, situated on the eastern slopes of the Troodos Mountains

Mountain Walks

The CTO has selected several interesting mountain walks for you. Each route is traced on a map and described in a pamphlet; each pamphlet also contains a chapter specially for bird-watchers. This interesting material is available at the Platres CTO office.

There is also a specialized and richly illustrated guide of the region, *Landscapes of Cyprus*, by Daniel Geoff, published by Sunflower Books.

Other sources of information on the region

are: *Flora of Cyprus*, volumes I and II (1977, 1985), R.D. *Cyprus Trees and Shrubs* (1949) – E.F. Chapman. *Flowers of Cyprus*, *Plants of Medicine*, volumes I & II (1987) – Chr. Ch. Georgiades.

It is not difficult to explore the landscape on your own; you will find the local folk very friendly and helpful. Indeed, you might even encounter a hunter or a mushroom picker as you stroll along.

We shall briefly outline some of the hiking routes.

The **first route** is also the longest: more than 6 miles (a 3-4 hour walk) on the Troodos-Prodromos Road; it climbs from Troodos up **Mt. Olympos** and to the TV aerials at its peak.

The Troodos Mountain trails offer a few charming spots for relaxation

Leave Troodos and follow the road for 2 miles to the picnic site. *Don't* follow the arrow sign to Mt. Olympos; the direct path, indicated by the arrow, is steep, difficult and much more demanding. Carry on to Chromion. You will find several observation points on the way: the first toward Limassol and Platres; another, closer to the summit, overlooks the Kykkos Monastery, Prodromos and Throni (where the tomb of Archbishop Makarios III is located).

From here, if you feel up to it, you can climb to the top of Mt. Olympos. At the Troodos-Prodromos Road, turn right onto the mountain path that leads to the top.

The **second route** leaves

Troodos south-eastward and ends at one of the most striking observation points in the whole region. It is less than a 4 miles walk (but don't forget the way back...). There are some benches just a few minutes' walk from Troodos, near an observation point overlooking Mt. Olympos. Cross the Pano Amiantos (Asbest) Mines; a little further on you will come to the observation point, which has a spectacular view of the mines, the port of Limassol, the Salt Lake and several villages. It is also a good spot for a picnic, equipped with pinewood tables and benches. Enjoy your rest, your picnic – and the view, and having rested, walk back to Troodos along the same path.

The **third route** is a short walk (little more than a mile!) along the Kryos Potamos stream to the **Caledonia Falls** (no relation whatsoever to the Niagara Falls...). Start southwestward from Troodos, on the Platres Road (not far from the summer cottage of the President of Cyprus). On the way down you will see a signpost "500 meters – Nature Trail Caledonian".

Platres, situated on the southern slopes of Mt. Olimpos and surrounded by pine forests

The trail is pleasant, the vegetation impressive, and the view is spectacular. You may either turn back, or proceed along the path to Platres, leading back to Troodos. From here you may catch a bus or hitch a ride. We don't advise climbing back: the path upward to Troodos reaches 2,000 feet in less than a mile!

All itineraries start from Troodos; if you are staying in Platres, you should first get a ride into Troodos.

From Troodos to Nicosia

The distance from Troodos to Nicosia is 50-65 miles, according to the different routes.

The main road is rather good, and leaves Troodos in an easterly direction to Pano Amiantos, turning northward to Kakopetria and Galata. Having climbed down the northern slopes, it continues straight to the capital. If you are not in a hurry, turn right 9 miles after Galata (and 5 miles before Astromeritis) to **Nikitari**. You may expect a very bumpy drive. After 3 miles you will get to the **Assinou Church** (a.k.a. Panagia Forviotissa – 12th century), with the most striking Byzantine frescoes on the island. To visit the church, you will need the help of the Nikitari priest.

On approaching Nicosia you will come across a detour (indicated by clear road signs), since a segment of the main road is located within Turkish territory and cannot be crossed.

A hunter in the mountains

The longer, but more interesting route climbs down from the mountains through Palaichori and the Machairas Monastery (see "The Troodos Plateau"), continuing eastward to Nicosia.

If you wish to stop at the **Tamassos archaeological site**, turn right 6 miles past Palaichori toward Klirou. Cross the village and Malounta, turning right at Arediou toward Episkopeion and Pera. At Episkopeion turn right once more to Politikon, and you will find yourself beside Tamassos (see "Around Nicosia").

After the visit, turn back to Episkopeion and Pera. Less than one mile after Pera you will reach the Nicosia Road. Turn left at the last 9 miles of the ride to the capital.

Typical Troodos shrubs and trees

NICOSIA (LEFKOSIA)

Nicosia, the capital of Cyprus and its largest city and business centre, has a population of about 170,000. Its atmosphere – modern and dynamic – is very different from the tranquility of the rest of the island's towns and villages. Nicosia is the seat of government and home to all major businesses, it also boasts the best shopping facilities in Cyprus.

The Archbishopric Palace, with the monument to Archbishop Makarios

The city is politically and historically divided: its northern section belongs to Turkish Cyprus. The border crosses its streets and alleys, and on many corners you will see small bunkers and guard posts manned with armed soldiers.

Historically, Nicosia is divided into an old city and a new city; but the political border splits the old city in two. The old city was once surrounded by a wall, only parts of which still remain. Its streets are but narrow alleys; its houses are old and rather neglected. Most buildings in the old city are protected by law, with plans for their periodical restoration. A small section (Laiki Yitonia – "The People's Neighbourhood") has already undergone restoration, and its narrow alleys, lined with small shops and restaurants, will give you an idea of what Nicosia was like three centuries ago. The new city spreads southward, with only an occasional high rise in its centre. The suburbs are wide residential quarters, with small cottages and private villas – and no apartment buildings. The main business centre is located in the new city, within the triangle formed by Stasinos, Makarios III and Evagora Sts.

Turkish Nicosia (or Lefkosa in Turkish) – is north of the dividing "Green Line". The difference between the Greek and Turkish sections, divided by the so-called "Green Line", is easily recognized. While the Greek new city, in the south, is modern and lively, Lefkosa is traditional in style and facilities. There are several Gothic structures, such as the Selimiye and the Bedesten Mosque or the Lapidary Museum. There are also a number of Ottoman style public buildings, such as the Arabahmet Mosque, the Büyük Han ("Great Inn"), the Kumarcilar Han (Gamblers' Inn) and the Sultan's Library.

The City Structure

The Old City, a rounded enclave in the centre of town, is clearly outlined by the remains of the ancient walls. Its southern section consists of the **Laiki Yitonia** neighbourhood – the heart of Nicosia, together with the three main shopping streets: Stasinos, Makarios III and Evagoras. West of this zone, the Pedieos river crosses the city from north to south. Beyond the river are the Engomi suburb, the *Ledra* hotel, and the airport (abandoned since the 1974 civil war).

How to Get There

By Air: Greek Nicosia has no operative airport today. The old one was partially destroyed in the 1974 war, and although it remains within the territory of Greek Cyprus, it has never been rebuilt.

Turkish Nicosia, or rather Lefkosa, is serviced by the small Ercan Airport, situated near the village of Tymvou, 6 miles east of the city.

By Land: The only highway on Cyprus joins Nicosia with Limassol, about 50 miles south-westward. The *K.E.M.E.K* bus line (Tel. 463989 in Nicosia and Tel. 05-363241 in Limassol) runs an hourly bus service between the two centres. The Nicosia terminal is on Dionysus Solomos Square.

The Larnaca main road runs westward for 12 miles before joining the Limassol-Nicosia highway. These 12 miles are often packed with hundreds of private vehicles, trucks and

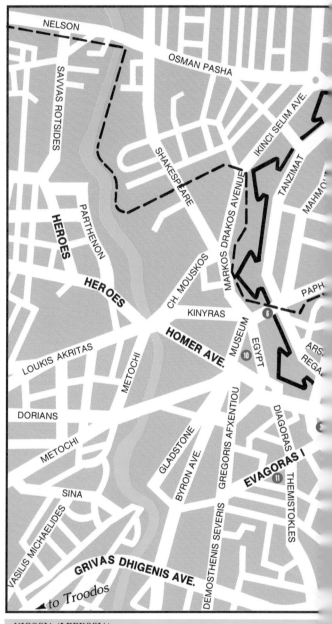

NICOSIA (LEFKOSIA)

1. Laiki Yitonia
2. Eleftheria Square
3. K.E.M.E.K. Terminal
4. Kellenos Terminal
5. Solomos Square Terminal
6. Pafos Gate

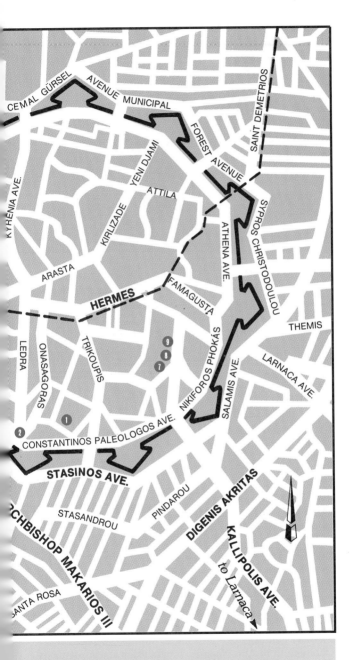

buses, bumper to bumper. At peak hours it is a very slow and nerve-racking drive.

Buses: *Kallenos*, Nicosia, Tel. 453560; Larnaca, Tel. 04-654890.

Taxi: *Acropolis Taxi*: 9 Stassinos Ave., Tel. 463456; *Amazon Taxi*: 48 Trikoupis St., Tel. 464383; *Columbia Taxi*: 59 Metochion Ave. Tel. 441700 (a 24 hour service).

Troodos is connected with Nicosia by two daily buses: the *K.E.M.E.K* bus (leaving Pano Platres at 6am, to Pedoulas and Nicosia); and the *Solea Bus* (6.30am from Troodos). Another *Solea Bus* line runs several times a day between Nicosia and Kakopetria.

The Agia Napa-Nicosia line offers a daily minibus ride – early morning from Agia Napa and mid-afternoon from Nicosia. The trip lasts about two hours.

Lefkosa – Turkish Nicosia – is connected by bus with Kyrenia (a 16 mile ride). Kyrenia is the Cypriot end of the Mersin (Southern Turkey) ferry service.

The only crossing open between Greek and Turkish Cyprus is the **Pafos Gate**, in the western section of Nicosia. Special visas are not required, but be prepared for lengthy and often unpleasant delays.

Tourist Services

The CTO office is in Laiki Yitonia, in the Old City (35 Odos Aristokypcou, Tel. 444264). Here you will find lots of written information on Nicosia and the rest of Cyprus, and the staff will assist you with information on cultural programmes and accommodation. The office is situated in a restored old residence, and it is not easily recognizable from the outside. Opening hours: September-May, Monday and Thursday 9am-5pm, Tuesday, Wednesday and Friday 9am-2.45pm, Saturday 9am-1.45pm; June-August, Monday and Thursday 9am-2.45pm and 4.30-6.30pm; Tuesday, Wednesday and Friday 9am-2.30pm and Saturday 9am-1.30pm.

The Main Post Office is also in Laiki Yitonia, across Constantinos Paleologos Ave., slightly west of the CTO (Tel. 303219). The Telephone Office is on Marcos Dracos Sq., near the Pafos Gate.

Bank branches are available everywhere; most common are the branches of Cyprus' two main banks: the *Bank of Cyprus* (the main office: 86-88-90 Phaneromeni St., Tel. 464064) and the *Popular Bank*. The Makarios III Ave. branches of both banks are also open for money-changing in the afternoon.

Urban Transportation

The urban bus transportation network reaches almost every corner of the city; its main terminal is on Solomos Sq, not far from Laiki Yitonia. Lots of private taxis cruise along all the main Nicosia streets, and can be hailed at will.

CAR HIRE

All major agencies have local branches in Nicosia.

Avis: 2 Homer St., Tel. 472062.

Europcar: 7E Santa Rosa St., Tel. 445201.

Hertz: 45B Grivas Digenis Ave. Tel. 477783.

A. Petsas: Ledra Hotel (Tel. 457457) and 24 Pantelides Ave., Tel. 462650.

Louis Self Drive Cars: 54-58 Evagoras St., Tel. 442114.

MOTORCYCLE HIRE

Agathria Trading Ltd.: 12A Bouboulina St., Tel. 474032.

Savvas Motorbike Ltd.: 23 Trikouppis St., Tel. 475680.

Bicycles can be hired at Tel. 455487.

Accommodation

The capital offers a wide choice of hotels of all classes, but only one apartment hotel, the B Class *Lordos* (18 Sina St., Engomi – more than a mile from the centre of town – Tel. 441039).

5-STAR HOTELS

Hilton: Makarios III Ave., Tel. 377777. The only 5 star establishment, very central and ideally located, adjacent to the access road leading to the Limassol highway. Luxury facilities, including swimming pool, tennis courts and sauna.

4-STAR HOTELS

Churchill Nicosia: 1 Achaeons St., Tel. 448858. Higher prices than most 4-star hotels. Centrally located, west of the Pedieos river. Facilities are adequate, but not comparable with 4-star hotels at seaside resorts.

Philoxenia: Eylenja Ave., Tel. 499700. Off-centre, south of the *Hilton*; wide range of services, pool, sauna and tennis courts.

Ledra: Griva Digheni Ave., Tel. 352086; west of the centre, quiet neighbourhood; swimming pool.

3-STAR HOTELS

Asty: 12 Prince Charles St., Tel. 473021. 4-star prices; at one mile from the centre. No swimming pool.

Europa: 16 Alceos St., Tel. 454537. West of the centre, near George Grivas Ave.

Excelsior: 4 Photiou Stavrou Pitta St., Tel. 368585. Central, near Santa Rosa Ave., one of Nicosia main streets.

Kennedy: 70 Regaena St., Tel. 475131. A modern building in the new city, outside the city walls. Roof swimming pool, with a splendid view of the city.

2-STAR HOTELS

Averof: 19 Averof St., Tel. 463447. East of the river, near the Green Line.

Nicosia Palace: 4-6 Pantelides Ave., Tel. 463719. Within the old city walls.

INEXPENSIVE HOTELS

City Sunhotel: 215 Ledra St., Tel. 463113.

Delphi: 24 Pantelides Ave., Tel. 457211. Central, within the old city walls; basic.

PENSIONS

Alasia: 23 Pigmalion St., Tel. 454384.

Femina: 114 Ledra St., Tel. 465729.

YOUTH HOSTELS

The Youth Hostel is across the street from the *Asty* hotel, 1.5 miles from the centre, at 13 Prince Charles St., Tel. 444808. Bus 27 from Solomos Sq. Open year round; office hours 7.30-10am and 4-11pm.

Restaurants

There are dozens of eating places in Laiki Yitonia, where you will find many *meze* restaurants, some with *bouzouki* bands. Often a waiter is posted at the entrance, to entice passers-by to venture in. One of the best, at 4 Solonos St., is the *Byzantine Palace*. Try the *stiffado*, it is excellent! (Tel. 477085). George Grivas Ave. is lined with restaurants, always packed with a local young crowd.

In the modern shopping centre situated at the corner of Makarios III Ave. and Agias Elenis St. you will find several pleasant cafés.

For cheap local cuisine and *meze* you may sample the *Kastri Tavern*, 9 Prokopian St., Tel. 496140, or the *Schistris Tavern*, 20 Aglantjias St., Tel. 335460.

Chang's China is an excellent Chinese restaurant, 1 Acropolis St., Engomi, Tel. 351350. Open 12.30am-3.30pm and 7.30pm-00.30am. It is recommended to make a reservation by phone.

Jewelry for sale in Nicosia

Mignon, 38 Metochiou Ave., Tel. 445032 (across the street form the *Churchill* hotel, offers French and British cuisine.

Kavouri is a seafood restaurant at 125 Strovolos Ave., tel 425153. Closed on Sundays.

Cellari, 17 Corais St., Tel. 448338 is a barbecue spot, with band.

Trattoria Romantica, 13 Evagoras Pallikarides St., Tel. 377276, is a good Italian restaurant.

The Indian Restaurant, 45 Prodromos St., Tel. 452183, is open 12am-2.30pm and 7-11pm; closed on Sunday. A choice of fifty traditional Indian entrées.

Pizza Parlours
Pizza Palace: 2 Acheon St.,
Makedonidissa. Tel. 351517.

Pizzarama: 1 Stasinou,
Engomi. Tel. 446368.

Shopping

The main shopping centre in
the old city is on Ledra St., a
narrow alley ending at an army
post, on the Green Line. The
street is lined with many small
shops, and some rather good
footwear outlets. There are
several handicraft shops,
selling copper, silver, earthenware, and lace.

For more attractive shop
windows, stroll along
Evagoras Ave., where you will
find *Benetton*, *Stefanel*, *Woolworth* and *Marks and Spencer*
outlets.

At the corner of Dhigeni
Akrita and Theodotou Sts.,
south-east of the old city, you
will find the open market.

Near the access road to the
Limassol highway, on 186
Athalassa Ave., there's an
Arts-and-Crafts Centre. Tel.
02-305024.

Night life

Most entertainment spots are
in Laiki Yitonia and west of
the centre, along George
Grivas Ave.

Behind the *Ledra* hotel there is
a ten-lane bowling alley,
always very crowded on
weekends. Not far from there
is the Nicosia International
Fair grounds.

In Engomi, slightly more than
a mile from the centre, there
are two discos: *Africana Disco*
(1a Michali Paridi St., Tel.
360435, open nightly), and
Scorpios Disco (3 Stassinos
St., Tel. 445967), the oldest of
Cyprus' discos.

The **Town Theatre** is very
central, near Museum St.; all

performances are in Greek. Tel. 463028.

Young people mostly frequent the Eleftheria Sq. pubs, but are also happy to stroll along the main shopping areas.

Sports
Six miles south-west of Nicosia there is a Sports Centre and a riding school.

Races are held regularly at Agios Dhometios, one of Nicosia's suburbs, one mile east of the town centre. Racing events are held on Sunday (June and July on Saturday); no races from mid-July to mid-September. The address of the *Nicosia Racing Club* is P.O.B 1783, Nicosia.

Tennis courts are available at most hotels, and also: *Champs Elisées:* Tel. 353188; two asphalt courts. *Eleon Tennis Club:* 3 Ploutarchous St., Engomi, Tel. 449923, 2 dirt courts and 7 asphalt courts.

Festivals
The annual Nicosia international fair is held on the last week of May. In September there is an arts festival.

Useful Phone Numbers

Nicosia area code: 02.
Police, first aid and fire brigade: Tel. 199.
Hospital: Homer Ave., Tel. 452760.
Municipality: Constantinos Paleologos Ave., near Eleftheria Sq.
CTO: 35 Odos Aristokyprou, Laiki Yitonia, Tel. 444264.

Music in Nicosia

Car breakdown emergency service: 12 Odos Chr. Mylona, Tel. 313131.

Self service laundromat: 12 Odos Prodromou, Tel. 472776.

British Embassy: 36 Alexander Pallis St., Tel. 471311.

USA Embassy: corner of Dositheos and Therissos Sts., Tel. 465151.

High Commission of Australia: 4 Odos Annis Komninis, Tel. 473001.

German Embassy: 10 Nikitaras St., Tel. 444362.

Swedish Embassy: Princess Zena de Tyra Palace, Tel. 442483.

Norwegian Embassy: 4 Metaxaki St., Tel. 472024.

Sites to See

We will start our walk from **Laiki Yitonia**, the quarter within the old city which has been restored. It is the pride of all Nicosians and the centre of the capital's life. Restoration began in 1981, and included renewal and reconstruction of all structures within the target area. Now the streets are lined with small art-and-crafts shows, boutiques and galleries. The project won the 1988 "Pomme d'Or", a prestigious biennial international prize.

The Panagia Phaneromeni Church

A leisurely stroll in the streets of Laiki Yitonia is highly recommended, both by day and by night; surrender to the invitation of one of the waiters beckoning you to enter his restaurant; sit down and enjoy a *meze* and the *bouzouki* band.

The CTO organizes a walk through the most fascinating monuments and narrow streets of Laiki Yitonia neighbourhood. The tours leave from the CTO office every Thurs. at 10am.

At 17 Ippokratous St. you will see the **Leventis Municipal Museum** (Tel. 451475). The building is a mansion characteristic of the end of the 19th century, very accurately restored. It houses an interesting presentation of daily Nicosian life throughout the ages. The museum is open Tuesday-Sunday, 10am-4.30pm. Free entrance.

From the museum turn right, and walk a short way on Onasagoras St., to the **Panagia Phaneromeni Church**. This fine Orthodox church was rebuilt on ancient remains at the end of the 19th century.

To visit the sites of the old city in the eastern quarter, turn back to Laiki Yitonia, and follow Constantinos Paleologos and Nikiforos

The Liberty Monument

Aves. along the inner side of the wall. After some 500 yards you will find yourself at the **Liberty Monument**, on the corner of Nikoforos Phokas and Koraes Sts. The monument commemorates the release of EOKA Cyprian patriots in 1959.

Turn left into Koraes St., following it to the corner of Kyprianos and Zenon of Kitium Sts.

Between these two streets you will find several interesting structures and sites. The first, to the south, is the **Archbishopric Palace**, a modern, impressive mansion, built in Byzantine style (1955-60).

North to the palace is the **Agios Ioannis Cathedral** (Greek Orthodox). Built in 1662 on the foundations of a 15th century Benedictine Monastery, its impressive interiors house a series of reproductions of 18th cen-

tury works of art. The most magnificent is the *Judgement Day*; you will find it above the southern door. Open Mon.-Sat. 8am-noon and 2-4pm. Entrance free.

Cross the inner court of St. John's Cathedral, and enter the **Cultural Centre of the Archbishop Makarios III Foundation**. The Centre houses the **Byzantine Museum**, whose very rich collection of statues, paintings and fragments date from a period ranging from the 8th to the 18th century. It depicts the development of decorative arts in Cyprus from their crudest Early Middle Age expression to their 12th century peak. The influence of European Crusaders, and later of Venetian traders, is evident. During the Ottoman period (16th-19th centuries) the figurative arts, and specially sculpture, were neglected and practically abandoned.

Part of the Liberty Monument

The museum is open Monday-Friday, 9am-1pm and 2-5pm (Saturday 9am-1pm). Tel. 366985.

Within the Cultural Centre you will find other museums as well: The first is the **Museum of the National Struggle**, dedicated to the war of independence against the British. Open Monday-Friday, 7.30am-2.30pm and 3-5.30pm. Entrance fee. Tel. 302465.

Next is a 15th century Benedictine monastery, housing the **Museum of Folk Art**. Its halls contain a collection of Benedictine relics, ancient farming tools, religious art objects, *Lefkaritika* and other lace and Foini earthenware (under renovation; Tel. 463205).

West of the old city, near the Pafos Gate, inside the City Gardens, is the **Cyprus Museum** (Stylianos Lenas Sq., corner of Museum St. and Homer Ave.). Walk along Homer Ave., outside the walls, from Eleftheria Sq. until you reach Stylianos Lenas Sq.

The Cyprus Museum, the most important archaeological museum in the country

Built in 1908, the Cyprus Museum is the most important archaeological museum on the island, and is highly recommended. It contains stone jars of the 6th millennium BC (from Choirokoitia), a marble statue of Aphrodites (from Soli, 1st century BC) and a gold sceptre (from Kourion, 11th century BC). Open Monday-Saturday, 9am-5pm, Sunday 10am-1pm. Tel. 302189.

Across the square are the **Botanic Gardens**, with an interesting collection of flowers, shrubs and trees.

The **Cyprus Handicraft Centre** is at 25 Demophontos St. It houses a permanent collection of handicrafts as well as a handicraft sales centre. Tel. 303065.

The **Museum of Modern Arts** is at the corner of Evagorou and Themistokli Dervi Aves.; open June-September, Monday-Friday, 10am-1pm and 4-7pm, Saturday 10am-1pm; the rest of the year Monday-Friday 10am-1pm and 3-6pm, Saturday 10am-1pm.

Around Nicosia

TAMASSOS

Leave Nicosia south-westward on the main road to Kato Lakatameia and Kato Deftera. Follow it until the Pera turnoff (on the right-hand side). Cross Pera and proceed to Episkopeion. Here turn left to Politikon.

Tamassos archaeological site

Before reaching this last village you will see the **Tamassos archaeological site** on your left.

In ancient times, Tamassos was one of Cyprus' main centres, surrounded by fertile farmland and rich copper mines. Its two main temples were dedicated to Apollo and Aphrodite. During the 1970's, the site of Tamassos was mapped and researched, bringing to light the foundations of several large structures and important fragments from the Sanctuary of Aphrodite. Not far from the site are also two burial caves, discovered in 1890 (a third cave was completely destroyed). These relatively well preserved caves have been attributed to the 7th century BC. The first and wider one contains a reconstructed porch and two burial rooms. The porch roof is supported by two columns decorated with Greek inscriptions. The ceilings are almost 8 feet tall, and the size of the rooms is approximately 9x10 feet. The second cave is similar to the first, only slightly smaller.

The site is open to visitors June-September, Tuesday-Sunday, 9-12am and 4-7pm; the rest of the year, 9am-1pm and 2-4.30pm; also closed on Monday. Entrance fee.

Entering one of the caves in Tamassos

THE ATHALASSA NATIONAL PARK

This is a 10 mile ride (by car or by bicycle). Leave Nicosia toward Limassol, but turn left at the highway entrance traffic lights. The road will take you to a pleasant park of pine, eucalyptus and cedar trees. If you secured a permit in advance (Tel. 02-403526), you may stop and fish at the dam.

DHALI

Leave Nicosia toward Limassol, either on the highway or on the old Limassol Road. Nine miles off Nicosia, take the left-hand turnoff to **Dhali**, a village built on the ruins of the ancient site of **Idalion**, on the southern side of the Valias river. According to myth, Idalion was founded by Khalcanor, one of the heroes of the Trojan war, who built 14 sanctuaries to Aphrodite, Apollo, Athena and other gods in his new citadel.

At the entrance to Dhali

The first survey of the site was carried out in 1865-1876 by the American consul Luigi Palma de Chensola, who discovered literally thousands of tombs, most of which were transferred to the **New**

York City Museum. Lower and earlier levels were later discovered, going back to the 17th century BC. Excavations also uncovered fragments of the 6th and 7th century BC city walls, as well as hundreds of coins, fragments and artifacts of the Aechean, Hellenistic and Roman periods.

A church in Dhali

TURKISH CYPRUS

Crossing to the Turkish Side

Crossing the "Green Line" from Greek Cyprus to the **TRNC (Turkish Republic of Northern Cyprus)**, the visitor will certainly feel the change in atmosphere. Not much has changed here since the 1974 war. The Turkish Cypriots may have gained independence, yet they thus became cut off from the western world. Nevertheless, a visit here can be quite an interesting experience, and there are some fascinating sites, such as Kyrenia (Girne), the St. Nicholas Cathedral and the archaeological site of Salamis.

The only crossing point is at Nicosia. With your valid passport in hand proceed to the Pafos Gate. The first thing you will see is a huge wall billboard, beckoning the tourist to visit the dilapidated and empty homes and the ruined sanctuaries – and never to forget 1974. Your name will be registered at the border control and you will be asked to reenter the Greek zone by 5pm (when the gate closes). You will then be asked to proceed to the Ledra Palace, the UN Peace Corps barracks and border post. On the palace walls dozens of old bullet holes are visible. On the Turkish side you will be asked to fill in another form, to pay a small sum and to present your passport.

One of the waiting taxis will be glad to take you to the centre of Lefkosa (Turkish Nicosia) or to any other site in Turkish Cyprus –

Girne Castle

such as Kyrenia for example. The centre of Lefkosa is less than a mile away, within easy walking distance.

A visit to Lefkosa will only take a few hours. In this chapter we will take you through its main (not very well preserved) sites, to the marketplace and to a pleasant and inexpensive lunch.

Note: you may not enter Turkish Nicosia with a rented vehicle. The use of a camera in this zone is not recommended. The purchasing of any item is prohibited.

If you plan a visit to other sites in Turkish Cyprus, you should cross the border in the early morning: the gate opens at 8am (and you must be back before 5pm. Failure to do so will automatically put you on the "missing persons" list, with all the unpleasant formalities this entails).

The local currency is the Turkish Lira, but CYP, $US and European currencies are always welcome.

Only tourists are admitted to Turkish Cyprus; the border is absolutely closed to Greek Cypriots.

Lefkosa – Turkish Nicosia

Lefkosa is a rather sorry sight. Its alleys are neglected and untidy; the houses are unattractive.

The **Turkish Museum** (Mevlevi Tekke) is near the Kyrenia Gate, in an early 17th century building, a former Dervish sanctuary.

In the **Berbers' Museum** you will find plentiful evidence of the continuous feud between Turkish and Greek Cypriots. The museum was the former family residence of Major Ilhan, who was killed in 1963 by EOKA fighters. Ilhan was a major in the Army

Medical Corps – the medical officer of one of the Turkish battalions. After his death he became a symbol of the Turkish struggle.

The **Selimiye Mosque** was built as the St. Sophie Cathedral in the de Lusignans period (13th century), in French Gothic style fashionable at the time. It was a joint project of Queen Alix de Champagne and of Archbishop Thiryx. After its consecration, it was used for the coronation ceremonies of the de Lusignan kings. The Ottoman conquerors transformed it into a mosque, adding three minarets to it and an offering table. However, the 14th century statues and reliefs of saints and angels on its doors and panels have survived, even if the mosque is used daily for Moslem rituals.

The Selimiye Mosque, built in the 13th century in French Gothic style

Near the mosque you will see the **Bedesten** (bazaar), a trade and handicraft centre, set up by the Ottoman conquerors in what used to be St. Nicholas of the English, a 14th century Greek Orthodox church, very popular during the Venetian period.

The **Lapidary Museum** is a 15th century Venetian building.

In the **Sultan Mahmoud II's Library**, built in 1829 by the Turk Governor Al Ruhi, you will find thousands of volumes from the great Sultan's private library. On the window sill of the small reading room you will see the Sultan's crest and signature. The library also contains later donations of books, side by side with the original library of Mahmoud II.

The **Obelisk** was brought to Lefkosa from

Salamis, in commemoration of the Venetian conquest of Cyprus which took place in the 15th century.

The **Büyük Han** (Great Inn) and the **Kumarcilar Han** (Gamblers' Inn) are two neighbouring and very similar Ottoman structures. The first is, of course, slightly larger and also older. It has an inner court for carriages, with a small mosque in its centre.

Tours in Turkish Cyprus

Two brief tours of Turkish Cyprus are outlined in the following tours; westward and eastward from the capital. Both tours start from Lefkosa and pass through Girne (Kyrenia). Each of the tours requires a full day, but keep in mind that you must be back at the border at 5pm at the latest (see "Crossing to the Turkish Side" p. 151).

The Western Tour

Lefkosa – Kyrenia – the western coast – Güzelyurt (Morphou in Greek) – Lefke – Nicosia. Total: little more than 100 miles.

At Lefkosa's market

Leave Lefkosa northward on the Kyrenia road; on the way you will pass the villages of Ortaköy and Gönyeli, and cross the Kyrenia Range (in Turkish Besparmak). Ten miles off Lefkosa, on the pass, turn left to the **Agios Ilarion Castle** (little more than one mile from the road). This castle is the best preserved of three Medieval fortresses situated along the Kyrenia Range (the others are the Kantara and the Buffavento Castles). It was built in the 10th century as the St. Ilarion Monastery, but was subsequently buttressed and

The well-preserved
Agios Ilarion Castle

transformed into a fortress. Today the ancient monastery is in ruins, but within its walls there is a relatively well-preserved Byzantine church, dating back to the 11th century. The battlements are armed with 9 turrets. Among the monastery ruins you will recognize the monks' quarters, the cellars, the summer residence of the de Lusignan family and St. Ilarion's tomb. Near the regal suite of the de Lusignans you will see a narrow building, whose styles reflect different periods.

Back to the main road, turn left, and after 3 more miles you will arrive in Kyrenia.

KYRENIA (GIRNE)

Before the 1974 war, this town used to be one of Cyprus' major tourist resorts, thanks to its excellent strategic position, in the centre of Cyprus' northern coastline and at the foot of the Kyrenia Range. Its hotels still remain, but are mostly deserted.

Kyrenia's first settlements date from 6,000 years ago. It is an archaeologist's paradise, with scores of sites to explore and dozens of mountain groves and sunny beaches to spend leisure time.

The Sites

The Venetians determined the present rectangular shape of the **Girne Castle** (Girne is Kyrenia). It served as their first defensive stronghold against the Ottoman threat. The Venetians built it on an old Byzantine fort, designed to check the 7th century wave of Arab expansion. You may enter through the modern bridge, from which a long corridor will take you to a section of the fort dating from the de Lusignan period (14th century). You may also enter the fort through a passage situated at the tomb of the Turkish admiral Sadik Pasa.

Girne Castle, built on an old Byzantine port

Today the fort houses Kyrenia's **Sailing Ships Museum**. Here you will find the remains of one of the most ancient boats ever recovered from the bottom of the sea. It dates back to the 4th century BC, sunk in the Kyrenia Bay, one mile off the harbour, at the time of Alexander the Great. You will also see part of the merchandise found in its holds, including 4,000 wine amphoras, scores of wooden tools, four oil amphoras and four salt containers, etc.

The **Museum of Arts** exhibits a collection of European modern art, various objects from the Far East, and Chinese and European porcelain.

The **Museum of Folk Art** is housed within a splendid residence, which is characteristic of the upper class 18th century Cypriots. The mansion is situated at the Kyrenia harbour, and it has three main levels. Its cellars were used as a storing area. The first floor used to house the services, kitchen and crafts area;

Kyrenia's Sailing Ships Museum

now it exhibits a collection of farming tools and looms. The second floor was the living area; the third was the bedroom floor, and here you will find a selection of home furnishing dating back to this period including bed linen, tablecloths, local embroidery and lace, as well as a collection of gold and silver objects.

Not far from the harbour you will find the mosque of **Cafer Paşa**, with its tall minaret – a splendid example of Ottoman architecture.

The Girne Castle served the Venetians as a defensive stronghold

AROUND KYRENIA

About 6 miles east of Kyrenia you will find the **Belapais Abbey**, a 12th century abbey in the Gothic style of the de Lusignan period. The abbey is built around an inner court, where the church, the dining room and the dormitory of the monks are located. It is also known as the **Blanche** (white) **Abbey**, probably because of the white habit worn by its monks. The abbey was erected by the Order of St. Norbert, one of the less known orders of the Middle Ages.

The building is very well preserved, and its dining room (30x90 feet), built by King Hugh IV of the de Lusignan dynasty, is one of the best examples of Cyprus' Gothic

Belapais Abbey

style. Several first rank figures of Cyprus' history are supposedly buried here, but their tombs have not yet been found. Above the entrance door the crest of the de Lusignans is displayed. From the six windows of the northern wall you will enjoy a most splendid view of the sea, framed by the Taurus peaks, in the Anatolian Peninsula.

WEST OF KYRENIA

After this brief visit to Kyrenia, follow the coastal road westward, toward **Güzelyurt**. After 12 miles the road turns left (south), crossing the village of Panagra, where you will see the road sign indicating Güzelyurt, a small town in the midst of Cyprus' famous lemon groves.

Güzelyurt means "beautiful land", and this small provincial town is indeed situated on one of Cyprus' most beautiful spots, whose

At the Belapais Abbey

fertile soil is covered in citrus groves and vineyards and blessed with endless freshwater springs. The produce of the lemon groves is mainly for export, either in fruit form or as bottled juice. The town itself has no major tourist sites; it owes its charm exclusively to nature. It has some attractive beaches, and even some casinos.

Proceed south-westward, crossing Prastion to the archaeological site of Soli and to the Vouni Palace. After 9 miles you will come to the town of **Lefke**, another fertile enclave not far from the Güzelyurt Bay. Near Lefke is one of Cyprus' old copper mines. North of Lefke, very near the coastal road, is the archaeological site of **Soli**.

Soli was founded in the 6th century BC by King Philohypros, whose adviser was none other than Solon of Athens. Only a few decades later the town fell, after a long siege, into Persian hands. Soli's best period was under Rome. The town was completely destroyed in 648 by the Arabs. As in other sites, the ruins served as building blocks for construction of another town – in this case Port Said, in Egypt (in the 19th century). The site was researched for the first time in 1929; the first finding was a Roman amphitheatre, a semi-circular chorus and a rectangular stage. The acropolis was uncovered several years later, together with the mosaic floor of a very early church.

The Gothic styled Belapais Abbey

Having visited Soli, proceed westward for 3 miles along the coastal road and you will come to the **Vouni Palace**, enclosed within a brick wall on the top of an 800 feet high hill. The palace was built in the 5th century BC, at the approximate time of the great Cypriot rebellion against the Persians. The building was erected by the town governor of Merion, to prevent further armed attacks by the Cypriot rebels. A few years later a **Temple of Athena** was erected on the palace grounds, together with a series of auxiliary buildings: residences, kitchens, store-rooms, and barracks. In total, the palace had no less than 147 rooms.

While the outer wall was made of bricks, the palace walls were made of stone. Most of the palace was destroyed by fire in the year 380, and it was never rebuilt.

BACK TO NICOSIA
Leaving the Vouni Palace, you will start out

One of Famagusta's rich architectural relics, the Church of Sts. Peter and Paul.

on your way back to Lefkosa, and through the Pafos Gate to Greek Nicosia. Follow the coast of the Güzelyurt Bay, crossing Güzelyurt itself; the main road from here to Nicosia crosses the border between Turkish and Greek Cyprus, and therefore it is closed to traffic. The alternative route is somewhat longer and not in the best possible condition. Three miles north of Güzelyurt on the Kyrenia road, in the vicinity of Kapouti (in Greek Kalon Chorion), turn right (eastward), passing through Skylloura and make your way toward Nicosia.

The distance from the capital is 13 miles at the most, but the need to avoid erroneously crossing the border will take you further north to Agios Ermalaos and, miles further, to Krini and the Kyrenia-Nicosia main road. Just six more miles, and you will reach Nicosia.

The Eastern Tour
Lefkosa – Famagusta (Gazi Maguza in Turkish) – Salamis – the Karpas Peninsula – the Kantara Fortress – Kyrenia (Girne) – Nicosia is approximately 125 miles.

Leave Lefkosa eastward on the main road to Famagusta. Take the northern route (the southern route crosses into Greek Cyprus, and therefore is closed to Famagusta traffic). The road crosses the rather flat and uninteresting Mesaoria plain, and after about 36 miles you will reach Famagusta.

FAMAGUSTA

Before 1974, Famagusta (for the Turks, Gazi Magusa), was the best known name in Cyprus, thanks to its deep-water harbour, its well-sheltered marina and the hotels lining the beach. Famagusta has been part of Turkish Cyprus since 1974, and the town has fallen into ruin. It stopped growing, tourists stopped coming, its hotels fell into disrepair; only the major historic sites have kept most of their appeal.

Famagusta has a very rich history, indeed the richest in all of Cyprus. It began as a small fishermen's harbour, but during the de Lusignan period it became the island's main port-of-call, with hundreds of ships anchoring there on the way to Europe, or to the Holy Land and on to the East.

The St. Nicholas Cathedral, a remnant from the 13th century de Lusignans

The sites

The **St. Nicholas Cathedral** was built in 1298 by the de Lusignans. It is undoubtedly one of the most impressive and best preserved churches in Cyprus. Several Kings of Cyprus (and of Jerusalem) were crowned in this church. When the Ottomans conquered the town from the Venetians, in 1571, the cathedral was transformed into a mosque, equipped with a minaret and an offering table, and renamed Lala Mustafa Paşa. It remains a mosque to this day.

The so-called **Venetian Walls** also belong to the de Lusignan period. They are 2.5 miles long

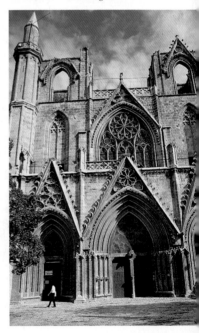

A winged lion guards the Othello Castle walls from past or prospect invaders

and enclose the entire old city. The walls were originally more than 6 feet thick, and were equipped with several turrets. With the introduction of artillery, in 1489, the Venetians decided to strengthen the walls, making them 60 feet tall and more than 20 feet thick. Outside the walls a moat was dug, and kept full of water at all times. There were two entrance gates, accessible by drawbridge. However, even that couldn't save Famagusta from the Turks, who conquered it in 1571 after four months of bitter fighting.

The **Othello Castle** is a second defensive fort, built by the de Lusignans in the 13th century; it was reinforced and expanded in the beginning of the 16th century by the Venetians. According to legend, this is where Cristoforo Moro, a high Venetian official in Cyprus during the years 1506-08, killed his beautiful but unfaithful wife Desdemona. The case inspired Shakespeare to write his play *Othello*. Hence, the present name of the castle.

Affront Namik Kemal Prison

The old **Church of Sts. Peter and Paul**, which was built in 1358, became the Sinan Paşa Mosque during the Ottoman period. Çelebi Mehmet Efendi, a Turkish diplomat of the 18th century, is buried in its court. After serving as his Sultan's ambassador in France he retired to Cyprus and died here in 1732.

The **Namik Kemal Prison** bears the name of a famous poet, imprisoned here from 1873-76 by the Sultan Abdul Aziz. Originally it was one of the royal residences of the de Lusignans.

The place was looted by the Turks in 1571, and its ruins were later restored as a police post and a small prison.

The **Canbolat Museum** contains an ethnographic collection of objects recovered in the town and its district. It bears the name of Canbolat Bey, a Turkish hero who fell in battle while defending the city, and is buried in the museum grounds.

The Othello Castle, built by the de Lusignans

SALAMIS

Salamis, 4 miles north of Famagusta, is one of the most important and magnificent archaeological sites on the island. The site of **Alasia**, one of Cyprus' most ancient settlements, is also in the same area.

Leave Famagusta on the Engomi road, along the coast. After 3 miles, turn left toward Engomi and Alasia. Alasia was an affluent settlement during the Bronze Age. Its name is mentioned in several Egyptian papyri. Archaeologists found gold and ivory ornaments, amphoras and Mycaenean earthenware in several of the tombs.

A statue in Salamis

Proceed further on, and after little more than half a mile turn right, toward the seashore. Having reached the coastal road, turn left for less than a mile, and you will see the site of **Salamis** on your right.

The mythological father of Salamis is Tefkros, another hero of the Trojan War, banned by his father, King of Salamis, who blamed him for the suicide of his brother Ajax. Tefkros landed, at what used to be known as the Akalar Beach, with a handful of faithful followers. As soon as he settled down, he built a temple to Zeus (whose ruins can be seen to this day in the southern section of the market), and gave his town the name of his childhood home, Salamis.

The town had an inner and an outer wall; fragments of the **inner wall** can be seen at the entrance to the site. An earthquake in the 4th century destroyed most of the buildings; the ruins of the Roman Amphitheatre were later used to build the **Turkish Baths**. The **amphitheatre**, with its spacious stage, can still be clearly identified. Along the stage you can see the trench used to collect blood from the victims consecrated to Dyonisus before each ritual. Only the first eight of the fifty rows of seats belong to the original Roman structure; the rest are later additions. In the *agora* (market place) a memorial stone bears witness to its inauguration in the year 22 BC.

THE KARPAS PENINSULA

Follow the main coastal road toward the north; after 9 miles, near Bogazi, you will come to the tip of the Karpas Peninsula, a long and narrow strip of hilly farmland pointing toward east-north-east. It is a region full of water sources and its sea-water teams with fish and other seafood. You will also find several hot-water springs on the peninsula as well as the **Kantara Castle** and the **Apostolos Andreas Monastery**. All this does not change the fact that this is one of the most deserted regions on the island.

The road proceeds along the peninsula well beyond Bogazi, for 36 miles, and ends at **Cape Andreas**, with the Apostolos Andreas Monastery and a lonely lighthouse. If you are short of time turn north at Bogazi, taking the mountain road that climbs the Bespar-mak Range (also called the Five Fingers); then turn right to stop briefly at the Kantara Castle.

The **Kantara Castle** is the last of the three fortresses built during the Byzantine period on top of the Kyrenia Range. It towers over the coastal strip from a height of 2,000 feet. It is almost inaccessible, and even after centuries of wars, during which it changed

Salamis, one of the most important archaeological sites in Cyprus

hands often, its walls and ramparts still remain almost perfectly preserved.

Proceeding westward and then northward from Kantara, you will reach the little town of Davlos, and the main coastal road. Follow it westward to **Belapais** and to the **Belapais Abbey**, which is described in the "The Western Tour". The road continues to Kyrenia, but you can turn back to Lefkosa and to the Pafos Gate to Greek Nicosia.

Belapais Abbey, dating back to the 12th century

INDEX

INDEX

NOTES

NOTES

NOTES

QUESTIONNAIRE

In our efforts to keep up with the pace and pulse of Cyprus, we kindly ask your cooperation in sharing with us any information which you may have as well as your comments. We would greatly appreciate your completing and returning the following questionnaire. Feel free to add additional pages.

Our many thanks!

To: Inbal Travel Information (1983) Ltd.
18 Hayetzira St.
Ramat Gan 52521
Israel

Name: _____

Address: _____

Occupation: _____

Date of visit: _____

Purpose of trip (vacation, business, etc.): _____

Comments/Information: _____

_____

_____

_____

_____

_____

_____

_____

INBAL Travel Information Ltd.
P.O.B 1870 Ramat Gan
ISRAEL 52117